Curtis's Botanical Magazine, Volume 84...

Sir William Jackson Hooker, David Prain, Otto Stapf, Bentham-Moxon Trust, Royal Horticultural Society (Great Britain), Royal Botanic Gardens, Kew, Stanley Smith Horticultural Trust

CURTIS'S BOTANICAL MAGAZINE,

COMPRISING THE

Plants of the Royal Gardens of Kew

AND

OF OTHER BOTANICAL ESTABLISHMENTS IN GREAT BRITAIN;
WITH SUITABLE DESCRIPTIONS;

BY

SIR WILLIAM JACKSON HOOKER, K.H., D.C.L. OXON.,

F.L.S., CORRESPONDING MEMBER OF THE ACADEMY OF SCIENCES OF THE IMPERIAL INSTITUTE OF FRANCE, AND DIRECTOR OF THE ROYAL GARDENS OF KEW.

VOL. XIV.
OF THE THIRD SERIES;
(*Or Vol. LXXXIV. of the Whole Work.*)

"Nature, enchanting Nature, in whose form
And lineaments divine I trace a hand
That errs not, and find raptures still renewed,
Is free to all men,—universal prize."

LONDON:
LOVELL REEVE, HENRIETTA STREET, COVENT GARDEN.
1858.

JOHN EDWARD TAYLOR, PRINTER.
LITTLE QUEEN STREET, LINCOLN'S INN FIELDS.

TO

THE COUNTESS OF DONERAILE,

DONERAILE, IRELAND,

A GREAT ADMIRER

AND SUCCESSFUL CULTIVATOR OF PLANTS,

The present Volume is Dedicated,

BY HER LADYSHIP'S

FAITHFUL AND OBEDIENT SERVANT,

THE AUTHOR.

ROYAL GARDENS, KEW,
Dec. 1, 1858.

V Fitch del. et lith
Vincent Brooks

Tab. 5025.

ANANAS bracteatus.

Scarlet Pine-apple.

Nat. Ord. Bromeliaceæ.—Hexandria Monogynia.

Gen. Char. Perigonii superi sexpartiti *laciniæ* exteriores *calycinæ* erectæ, interiores *petaloideæ* erectæ, ligulatæ, basi intus bisquamosæ, squamis tubulosis. *Stamina* 6, epigyna, perigonii laciniis interioribus opposita; *filamentis* inter earundem squamas retentes, *antheris* linearibus erectis. *Ovarium* inferum, triloculare. *Ovula* in placenta palmatifida, ex apice anguli centralis loculorum protuberante pendula. *Stylus* filiformis; *stigmata* 3, carnosula, erecta, fimbriata. *Baccæ* inter se et cum bracteis in syncarpium conferruminatæ, loculis plerumque abortivis aspermis, rarissime bi-triloculares. *Semina* in loculis solitaria, ex apice loculorum pendula, ovoidea, compressiuscula, *testa* membranacea, fusca, striata, *rhaphe* fasciæformi alba umbilicum basilarem chalazæ apicali tuberculiformis jungente. *Embryo* minimus, in basi albuminis farinacei rectus, extremitate radiculari umbilicum attingente, supera.—Herbæ *Americanæ* (?) *per tropicos totius orbis diffusæ;* foliis *linearibus integerrimis vel spinuloso-serratis;* florum *spica densa, demum carnosa, connata, sæpe coma foliorum terminata. Endl.*

Ananas *bracteatus;* foliis spinoso-serratis, bracteis foliaceis coloratis. *Lindl.*

Ananasa bracteatus. *Lindl. Bot. Reg. t.* 1081.

Ananas bracteatus. *Ræm. et Schult. Syst. Veget. v.* 7. *p.* 1286.

Nana, *seu* Ananas. "*Marcgraaf, Hist.* 1. *cap.* 16 *(excl. ic.).*"

"Scarlet-leaved Pine. *Hortulan.*"

Highly ornamental a plant as this is to our stoves in the summer months, it is nevertheless doubtful to us if it should be considered in any other light than one of many varieties of the Common Pine-apple (*Ananas sativus*). That species is indeed characterized by the flowers "coma terminati." Even in our plant there is an incipient "coma," which in Dr. Lindley's figure *l. c.* is more fully developed. Our plants have not yet produced eatable fruit; but we are informed by Dr. Lindley that "the great merit of this species (*Ananas bracteatus*) consists in the clear deep crimson bracteæ of the flowering spike, which retain their colour, although less brilliant in the ripe fruit; *the latter, however, is so good, that no collection of Pines should be without the species.*"

January 1st, 1858.

Great allowance must be made for the variation in plants that have been for centuries under cultivation, especially in the case of esculent and fruit-bearing ones, and the kinds bearing fruit so much an object of competition, that there seems to be no end of forms and colour. This species has nothing to do with *Bromelia bracteata*, Sw. and of 'Hortus Kewensis.'

Seeing that, as far as our knowledge extends, there are no real differences between the two and *Ananas sativus*, already figured in this work, we abstain from any full description. Rœmer and Schultes express a doubt whether this be distinct from *Ananas Sagenaria* (Bromelia Sagenaria, "*Arruda de Camara, Diss.*," etc., p. 41), noticed too in Koster's Travels, vol. ii. p. 458. Both are considered natives of Brazil. With the latter we are totally unacquainted. Is there really more than one species of *Ananas*, or *true* Pine-apple?

Fig. 1. Portion of a leaf and a flower spike, *nat. size*. 2. Flower within its bractea and upon its fleshy receptacle. 3. Petal and stamen:—*magnified*.

5026.

W. Fitch del. et lith. Vincent Brooks Imp.

Tab. 5026.

SONERILA speciosa.

Showy Sonerila.

Nat. Ord. Melastomaceæ.—Triandria Monogynia.

Gen. Char. (*Vide supra*, Tab. 4978.)

Sonerila *speciosa;* herbacea erecta, ramis obtuse tetragonis, foliis longiuscule petiolatis cordato-ovatis acutis argute serratis 5–7-nerviis serratis glabris, petiolis versus apicem villosis, pedunculis terminalibus solitariis dichotomis, ramis demum elongatis scorpioideis, floribus secundis, calyce urceolato glanduloso-piloso, petalis subrotundo-ovatis mucronulatis carina dorso villosa, staminibus stylum æquantibus, antheris basi cordatis longiuscule acuminatis, dorso basi medio obtuse calcarato.

Sonerila speciosa. *Zenker, Plant. Ind. Nilgh. p.* 18. *t.* 18. *Ann. Sc. Nat. v.* 6. *p.* 151. *Wight, Ic. Plant. Ind. Or. t.* 2952.

From the collection of the Messrs. Veitch, of the Exeter and Chelsea Nurseries, who introduced the plant from the Neilgherries, at the same time with the *Sonerila elegans*, figured from the same collection at our Tab. 4978. It is a species that was quite unknown to M. Naudin, when he published his elaborate 'Melastomacearum quæ in Museo Parisiensi continentur Monographicæ descriptionis et secundum affinitates distributionis Tentamen.' It is a most lovely species, in richness of the colour of the flowers far exceeding the yet handsome *S. elegans* just alluded to. Zenker gives the locality of the plant about Otacamund; Dr. Wight, "Kaitie Falls, on moist sides of ravines above the Avalanche Bungalow, very abundant, flowering in February:" Dr. Wight seems to be alluding to the Neilgherries on the occasion.

Descr. *Stems* scarcely a foot high, moderately branched: *branches* herbaceous, obtusely quadrangular, glabrous. *Leaves* opposite, petiolate, cordato-ovate, acute, serrated, five- to seven- or even nine-nerved, glabrous. *Petioles* rather shorter than the leaf, channelled on the upper side, villous towards the extremity. *Peduncle* terminal on the branches, solitary, very glandulosely hairy, terete, bearing a bifid *cyme* of large deep rose-coloured flowers: the *branches* are subscorpioid and the *flowers* secund. *Calyx* urceolate and, as well as the *pedicels*, glanduloso-pilose; *limb* of three, patent, subrotund but acute lobes. *Stamens*, as in the genus, three. *Filaments* flexuose. *Anthers* cordate at the base, attenuated at the apex: on the back, at the point of insertion on the filament, is a short blunt spur. *Style* as long as the stamens, declined.

Fig. 1. Calyx, including the adherent ovary. 2, 3. Stamens:—*magnified.*

W. Fitch del et lith.

Vincent Brooks Imp.

Tab. 5027.

CORDIA IPOMŒÆFLORA.

Ipomœa-flowered Cordia.

Nat. Ord. Boragineæ.—Pentandria monogynia.

Gen. Char. *Calyx* tubulosus, obovatus campanulatusve, 4–5-dentatus, rarius 3- seu 6–8-dentatus. *Corolla* infundibuliformis vel hypocraterimorpha, limbo 4–8-partito, rarius 6–12-lobo. *Stamina* tot quot lobi, corollæ tubo inserta. *Stylus* bis bifidus, sæpius exsertus. *Drupa* ovata aut globosa, pulposa, calyce persistente sæpius cincta, nunc in ovario 4-locul. post anthesin abortu ad loculos 1–3 sæpe reducta, loculis 1-spermis.—Arbores *aut* frutices *regionum orbis calidarum incolæ.* Folia *alterna aut rarissime subopposita, petiolata, forma varia, integerrima aut dentata.* Flores *dispositione varii, interdum abortu polygami aut monoici.* Corollæ *fere omnium albæ. DC.*

Cordia (§ sebestenoides) *ipomϾflora;* arborea, ramis teretibus, petiolis elongatis pedunculis calycibusque subtus minute pubescenti-scabriusculis, foliis pedalibus–sesquipedalibus late obovato-lanceolatis acutis vix acuminatis dimidio superiore grosse spinuloso-dentatis, panicula terminali ampla laxa pluries dichotoma, floribus sessilibus, calyce urceolato-cylindraceo apice 2-trifido (siccitate substriato) ante anthesin apice conico-mucronato, corollæ (albæ) amplæ infundibuliformi-campanulatæ plicatulæ lobis rotundatis, staminibus 5, filamentis inferne hirsutis.

Similar as this fine *Cordia* unquestionably is to the *C. superba* figured at our Tab. 4888 (supposed to be a Brazilian species) it is nevertheless truly distinct. In our stove the plant is quite arborescent, having, though confined in a pot, attained a height of fourteen feet. The leaves are opaque (never nitent), a foot and more in length, with petioles two to three inches long; their apex is acute, not suddenly and finely acuminated, and the margins of the upper half are coarsely though irregularly dentato-serrate with large pungent spinulose teeth. The flowers are laxly paniculated, and though of the same shape and colour as in *C. superba,* are more than one and a half as large again, and resemble at first sight those of some white *Convolvulus* or *Ipomœa,* quite conspicuous at a considerable height from the ground.

January 1st, 1858.

It is to be regretted that, as was the case with the plant we figured for *C. superba*, we know nothing of its native country or introduction; and only that it is an old inhabitant of the warm stove in the Royal Gardens of Kew, with the blossoming of which, during the sunny season of the summer of 1857, we could not fail to be struck. The section of the extensive genus *Cordia* (now that nearly all the *Varroniæ* are included in it) to which this species belongs, is undoubtedly § *Sebestenoides* (Cordiæ macranthæ, *Cham.*), including twelve species, some inhabitants of the Old, some of the New World, none of them in characters according with the present species.

Descr. A small *tree*, as cultivated with us, twelve to fourteen feet high, probably, in its native country, like the *C. macrophylla* of Jamaica, forty to fifty feet; much branched, *branches* terete, brownish from close-pressed minute villous down. *Leaves* much confined to the branchlets, on terete *petioles* two to three inches long, obovato-lanceolate, a foot to sixteen inches in length, five inches wide in the broadest part, acute or only shortly and gradually acuminate, opaque on the surface (not glossy), tapering below gradually into the petiole, the upper half has the margins very coarsely dentato-serrate, the teeth unequal in size, and spinulose or mucronulate; glabrous above, petioles and younger leaves obscurely pubescent on the midrib and some of the principal prominent veins beneath. *Panicle* large, terminal. *Peduncle* and *pedicels* as well as the *calyx* downy; the latter sessile and subsecund on the branchlets, cylindrical or suburceolate, in bud conical and apiculate at the point; *limb* of two or three unequal short spreading lobes. *Corolla* one and a half inch in diameter, in form between infundibuliform and campanulate, white or yellowish-white, wrinkled (plicate): the *limb* of five large rounded spreading lobes. *Stamens* five, inserted near the base of the corolla, shorter than the tube; *filaments* hairy at the base; *anther* oval, cordate at the base. *Ovary* subrotund, four-celled, (each cell with one ovule), tapering upwards into a bifid *style*, each with a three-lobed *stigma*.

Fig. 1. Base of a corolla laid open, with stamens and pistil. 2. Transverse section of an ovary:—*magnified.*

5028.

W Fitch del. et lith. Vincent Brooks Imp

Tab. 5028.

GRAMMATOCARPUS volubilis.

Twining Grammatocarpus.

Nat. Ord. Loasaceæ.—Polyadelphia Polyandria.

Gen. Char. *Calyx* tubo lineari cum ovario connato, *limbi* superi quinquepartiti *laciniis* æqualibus. *Corollæ petala* 10, summo calycis tubo inserta, quinque ejusdem laciniis alterna, cucullata, basi subsaccata, majora, quinque iisdem opposita multo minora, apice bicallosa, triaristata. *Stamina* plurima, cum petalis inserta, *exteriora* sterilia acuminata conica granulata, petalis minoribus per paria opposita, *interiora* fertilia, in fasciculos 5, iisdem majoribus oppositos approximata; *filamenta* filiformia; *antheræ* biloculares, longitudinaliter dehiscentes. *Ovarium* inferum, uniloculare, placentis parietalibus tribus, nerviformibus. *Ovula* plurima, pendula, anatropa. *Stylus* simplex; *stigma* acutum. *Capsula* linearis, torta, limbi calycini reliquiis coronata, unilocularis, juxta totam longitudinem trivalvis, valvis margine seminiferis. *Semina* plurima, subglobosa; testa fibrosa, reticulata. *Embryo* in axi albuminis carnosi orthotropus; *radicula* umbilico proxima.—Herba *Chilensis, volubilis, pubescens;* foliis *oppositis, pinnatisectis;* floribus *axillaribus terminalibusque, solitariis, subsessilibus, flavis. Endl.*

Grammatocarpus volubilis.

Grammatocarpus volubilis. *Presl, Symb. Bot. v.* 1. *p.* 59. *t.* 38. *Walp. Repert. Bot. Syst. v.* 2. *p.* 255, *et v.* 5. *p.* 778.

Scyphanthus elegans. *Don, in Sweet Brit. Fl. Gard. v.* 3. *t.* 238. *Paxton, Mag. of Bot. v.* 10. *p.* 3, *cum ic. Gay, Fl. Chil. v.* 1. *p.* 465.

Loasa striata. *Meyen, Reise um die Erde, v.* 1. *p.* 310.

Descr. *Stems* long, slender, climbing and twining, herbaceous, slender, soon becoming brown, but not woody, frequently branched in a somewhat dichotomous manner, rough with minute deflexed and probably (like its congeners) stinging hairs. *Leaves* opposite, also rough with the like hairs; the lower ones bipinnatifid; upper ones smaller and only pinnatifid, sometimes trifid; all the segments oblong, uninerved. *Petiole* short, channelled. *Flowers* in reality sessile, but appearing peduncled from the narrow elongated pedunculiform inferior *ovary*, terminal or axillary and often arising from a fork of the branch. *Calyx-tube* very long, slender, terete and furrowed, incorporated with the ovary; *limb* of five, spreading, spathulate, leafy segments. *Petioles* yellow, five inserted at the very base of the calyx-segments, ascending so as to form a cup: each one obovato-spathulate, deeply saccate below the middle. *Scales* five, cucullate, at the apex having a lobed, red callosity, and three long horns or filaments. *Stamens* and *pistil* as described in the above generic character. The *fruit* we have not seen.

Fig. 1. Petal. 2. Scale with its three horns, callous apex, and with two stamens at the base within:—*magnified.*

5029.
2.
4.
W. Fitch del. et lith.
Vincent Brooks Imp

Tab. 5029.

COSMANTHUS GRANDIFLORUS.

Large-flowered Cosmanthus.

Nat. Ord. Hydrophyllaceæ.—Pentandria Monogynia.

Gen. Char. Calyx quinquepartitus, sinubus nudis. *Corolla* late campanulata, caduca, 5-fida, tubo esquamato, lobis æstivatione quincunciali. *Stamina* 5, filamentis gracilibus, corollam subæquantibus. *Pollen* oblongum. *Nectarium* minimum. *Ovarium* basi excepta pilosum, 5-loculare, placentis 2 parietalibus dorso liberis 2–8-ovulatis. *Stylus* bi-(tri-)fidus. *Capsula* valvis 2 medio septiferis dehiscens. *Semina* 4–10, ovoideo-angulosa, lateraliter aut rarius extremitate adfixa, rugulosa. *Embryo* (ex *C. parviflora*) minimus, *radicula* supera.—Herbæ *graciles, Boreali-Americanæ, annuæ*; foliis *alternis;* racemis *elongatis, ebracteatis, simplicibus;* floribus *pedicellatis, parvis, albis vel pallide cæruleis.*—Differt a *Phacelia* et *Eutoca* tubo corollæ nudo; ab *Emmenanthe* præterea corolla caduca. *Benth.*

Cosmanthus *grandiflorus;* adscendens, foliis lato-ovatis dentatis basi subcordatis rugosis uti caules et calyces hispidis, racemis ad apicem pluribus circinatis, calycibus subsessilibus, placentis ultra 50-ovulatis. *Benth.*

Cosmanthus grandiflorus. *Benth. in De Cand. Prodr. v.* 9. *p.* 297.

Eutoca grandiflora. *Benth. in Trans. Linn. Soc. v.* 17. *p.* 278.

Eutoca speciosa. *Nuttall, Plant. Gambel. p.* 158.

This plant has probably the largest flowers of all of the Order *Hydrophyllaceæ*. Although discovered by Mr. Douglas during his wanderings in California before 1834, it appears only lately to have been introduced to our gardens by Messrs. Veitch, through their collector Mr. William Lobb. We saw it for the first time flowering in the extensive, hardy herbaceous ground of Mr. Borrer, at Henfield, and thence obtained the specimens here figured. Mr. Nuttall detected the species at San Diego, California, and considering it to possess characters different from those of *Eutoca* (Cosmanthus) *grandiflora*, he described it under the name of *Eutoca speciosa*. Only a solitary specimen was received by the Horticultural Society from Mr. Douglas; but we possess fine native specimens in the herbarium from Mr. Nuttall and from Mr. William Lobb (n. 389), gathered on mountains of San Bernardino, South California. If the flowers possessed the rich blue colour of *Eutoca viscida*, it would indeed be a splendid ornament to our flower-borders.

Descr. A bold, free-growing, somewhat decumbent, herbaceous, branching *plant;* in its native country three to five feet high (*W. Lobb*), everywhere clothed with short simple hairs, intermixed with glandular and viscid ones, which Mr. Nuttall observes emit (when rubbed) a heavy, resinous, rather disagreeable smell, not unlike that of Rue. *Branches* terete, ascending. *Leaves* large, rather coarse, on short *petioles*, ovate, somewhat cordate at the base, sometimes approaching to rhomboid or triangular, doubly dentate, sometimes almost lobed at the margin, penninerved, nerves very prominent beneath. *Flowers* terminal on young superior branches, which (the leaves becoming gradually smaller) constitute a sort of leafy *panicle* of flowers. *Racemes* scorpioid. *Pedicels* very short, erect, so that the calyx is appressed to the rachis. *Calyx* cut into five, deep, linear, spreading, afterwards erect, segments, about as long as the tubular portion of the corolla. *Corolla* very large, almost two inches across, campanulato-rotate, purple (very pale externally), with a dark-purple ring and radiating lines at the faux. *Lobes* subrotundate, very obtuse; *tube* white. *Stamens* five, much exserted. *Anthers* oblong; *filaments* subulate, hairy at the base. *Ovary* pyramidal, partially villous. *Style* short, trifid; branches equal in length to the filaments of the stamens.

Fig. 1. Stamen. 2. Pistil:—*magnified*.

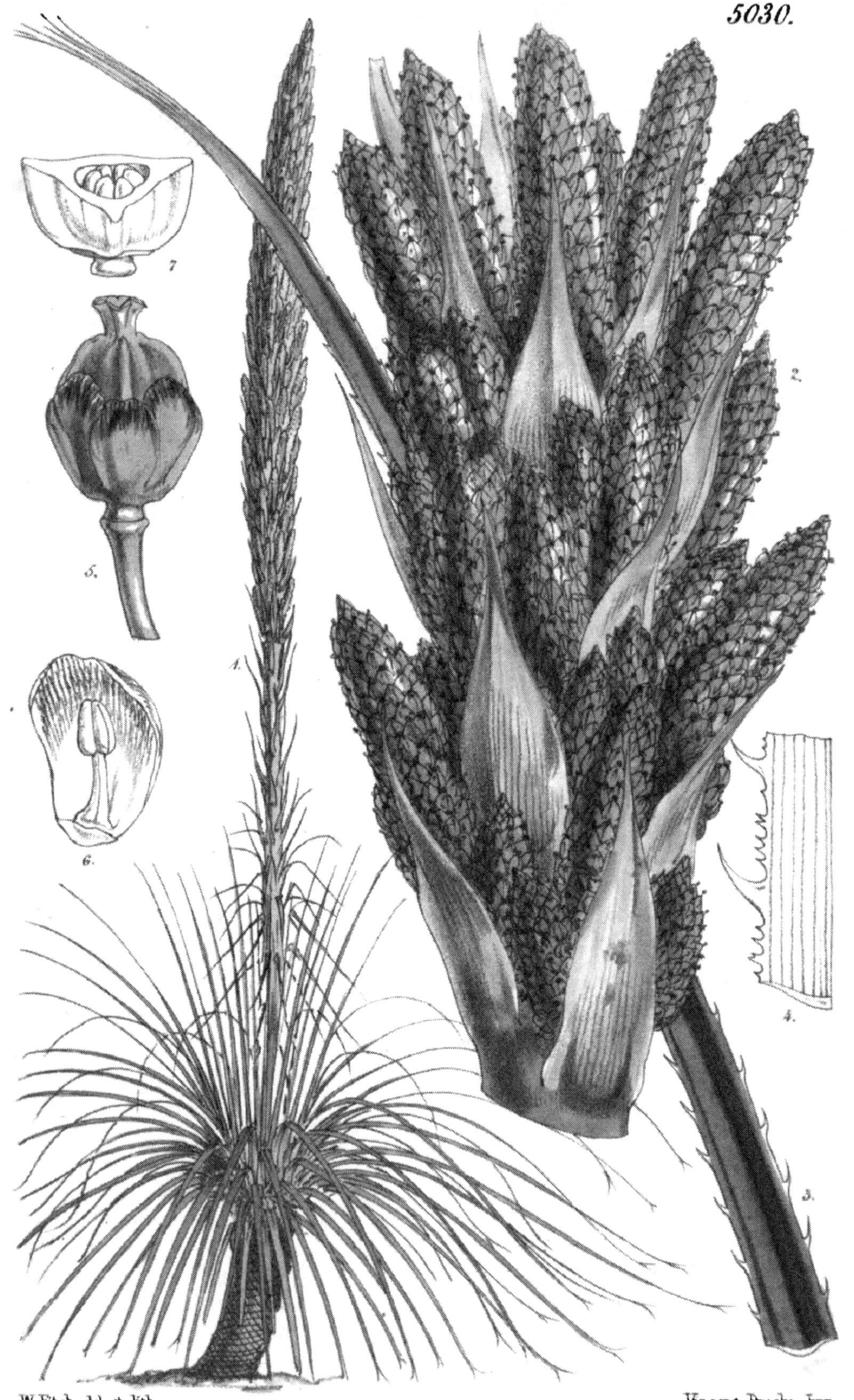

W. Fitch del. et lith.

Vincent Brooks Imp.

Tab. 5030.

DASYLIRIUM acrotrichum.

Bearded-leaved Dasylirium.

Nat. Ord. Asparagineæ.—Diœcia Hexandria.

Gen. Char. Flores dioici. Masc. *Perigonium* corollaceum, profunde 6-partitum; *foliolis* oblongis, uninerviis, navicularibus, campanulato-conniventibus (patentibus, *Brongn.*); exterioribus paulo longioribus vel brevioribus; præfloratio imbricata. *Stamina* sex, basi foliolorum inserta, plerumque iis breviora. *Filamenta* filiformia. *Antheræ* biloculares, oblongæ, utrinque bilobæ, dorso medio affixæ, introrsæ. *Pistillum* rudimentarium. Fl. Fœm. *Perigonium* maris. *Stamina* antheris effetis; *ovarium* liberum, triquetrum, angulis membranaceis, uniloculare; *ovula* 6, per paria approximata, fundo ovarii affixa, erecta, anatropa. *Columna stylina* brevis, in *stigma* infundibulare margine undulato-plicatum irregulariter lobatum dilatata (*stigma* trilobum; lobis brevibus, ovatis, divergentibus, *Brongn.*). *Fructus* nucumentaceus, abortu monospermus (*akenium*, Brongn.), ovato-trigonus, angulis in membranam latam expansis. *Semen* immaturum erectum, fusiforme, utrinque acutum. *Caulis* lignosus, abbreviatus, foliosus, vel elongatus, caudiciformis, apice foliosus, erectus.—Folia *e basi semiamplexicauli linearia, superne subulato-angustata, apice marcido sæpe* (*semper*, Brongn.) *in fila dissolubilia, canaliculata, striata, rigida, margine nunc spinosa, inter spinas denticulato-spinulosa, nunc scabra.* Paniculæ *terminales, solitariæ, erectæ, simplices vel ramosæ, bracteatæ.* Flores *parvi, albi, pedicellati, solitarii vel per 2–4 fasciculato-congesti, in ramulis spicati vel racemosi;* pedicellis *basi bracteolatis, superne articulatis.* Antheræ *flavæ.*

Dasylirium *acrotrichum;* caulescens, trunco elongato, foliis longissimis e lata basi lineari-subulatis viridibus fasciculo fibrarum emarcidarum terminatis planiusculis striatis rigide serrulatis spinosisque, spinis subulatis sursum curvatis, spica longissima cylindraceo-acuminata composita, spiculis (plant. fœm.) seu racemis cylindricis copiosis dense compactis erectis multifloris, bracteis amplis subæquilongis ovatis acuminatissimis, floribus (fœm.) dense imbricatis.

Dasylirium acrotrichum. *Zuccar. in Otto et Dietr. Allgem. Gartenz.* 1838, *n.* 33. *p.* 259. *Kunth, Enum. Pl. v.* 5. *p.* 40.

Yucca acrotricha. *Schiede in Linnæa, v.* 4. *p.* 230, *et n.* 6. *p.* 52. *Schultes, Syst. Plant. v.* 7. *p.* 1716.

Roulinia acrotricha. *Brongn. in Ann. des Sc. Nat. v.* 14. *p.* 320.

Dasylirion gracile. *Hort. Berol.* 1847.

Of late years the greenhouses of botanic gardens have exhibited noble specimens of a very singular set of plants, with much of the habits of very narrow-leaved Yuccas, the foliage generally terminated with a pencil or brush of loose parallel rather rigid fibres, now and then sending up a solitary central stem of very small Asparagineous diœcious flowers, of which Zuccarini, in 1842, constituted a genus, to which he gave the not very appropriate name of *Dasylirium* (thick or succulent Lily). Some well-grown species adorn the south end of the long succulent-house of the Royal Gardens; and, probably on account of the unusually warm and sunny summer, two of the species threw up their noble flower-stalks, the present one so tall, that the flowering portion soon came in contact with the loftiest part of this house, and it had to be removed into a taller one to perfect its flowering. The genus being (it is stated) always diœcious, we have in the present instance only the female plant. All the kinds (and six are described, though imperfectly so in most cases) are considered to be natives of Mexico, and in their native mountains must form, along with *Cactuses*, a remarkable feature in the scenery. Our plants of this were received from Mr. Repper, of Real del Monte, through the kindness of the Company bearing that name.

Descr. *Stem* erect, or nearly so; in the individual under consideration about two feet high, and a foot at least or a foot and a half in girth, clothed with the broad, scale-like, withered bases of former years, and crowned by a graceful tuft of slender, pliable, but firm and coriaceous *leaves*, from three to four feet in length, the older and lower ones spreading and recurved, the younger and upper ones erect; all, from a broad base, rather suddenly linear-subulate, terminated by a harsh tuft or pencil of coarse fibres, nearly plane, that is, only slightly channelled on the upper surface, of an ordinary rather yellowish-green colour, finely striated on both sides, of a firm coriaceous texture, but with a graceful downward curvature of the old and lower leaves, the younger and terminal ones erect; the margins cartilaginous, white, and pellucid, cut into very fine sharp serratures, the teeth sometimes double, and beset with strong subulate spines, at distances of about half an inch, more or less, a line long, curved upwards, and of a pale-brown colour, the younger ones colourless. *Peduncle* terminal, solitary, at first rising up somewhat like a head of asparagus, but clothed with erect, imbricated, young leaves; then rapidly increases in size, and attains a height, including the flowers, of fifteen and sixteen feet, the lower part partially clothed with small leaves, which gradually pass upwards into subulate bracteas, and among the spikelets they are large, broad, membranaceous, ovate, sharply acuminated, brownish-green *bracts*, as long as or longer than the spikelets. *Spike* (female) three to four feet long, cylindrical, but slightly acuminated, loaded with the numerous, erect, bracteated *spikelets*, or more properly *racemes*. *Pedicels* short, jointed a little below the flower, and there deciduous. *Perianth* of six, erect, imbricated, concave, broad-ovate *sepals*, of a greenish colour, streaked with red at the apex, each enclosing an abortive stamen, shorter than the sepal. *Ovary* (abortive) larger than the sepals, orbicular-oval, with three thick but wing-like angles, and crowned with a deeply three-parted *style*. *Stigmas* triangular. *Cell* solitary, with three erect ovules.

Fig. 1. Entire plant, *much reduced in size*. 2. Small portion of a female flower-spike, *nat. size*. 3. Apex of a leaf, *nat. size*. 4. Portion of a leaf, *nat. size*. 5. Female flower. 6. Sepal, including the abortive stamen. 7. Transverse section of an ovary :—fig. 5 and 7 *magnified*.

W Fitch del et lith | Vincent Brooks Imp

Tab. 5031.

ÆSCHYNANTHUS tricolor.

Three-coloured Æschynanthus.

Nat. Ord. Cyrtandraceæ.—Didynamia Angiospermia.

Gen. Char. *Calyx* tubulosus, 5-dentatus, 3-fidus vel 5-partitus, subæqualis aut subbilabiatus. *Corolla* infundibuliformis, tubo subincurvo ad faucem ampliato, limbo obtuse trilobo irregulari subbilabiato. *Stamina* 4–5, inclusa, 2–3 sterilia, minima, 2 fertilia; antheris crassis, loculis parallelis. *Stigma* obtusum aut emarginatum. *Bacca* oblonga aut ovata, corticata, bilocularis, septi lobis in margine revoluto seminiferis. *Semina* plurima, nuda, sæpe foveata aut punctata.—Suffrutices *aut* herbæ, caule *erecto aut procumbente.* Folia *opposita, nunc æqualia, nunc altero abortivo pseudo-alterna.* Flores *fasciculati aut capitati aut solitarii, axillares, bracteati.* Corollæ *purpureæ (coccineæ), albæ, rarius flavescentes, imo luteæ. De Cand.*

Æschynanthus *tricolor;* scandens radicans subpubescens, ramis herbaceis teretibus, foliis brevi-petiolatis oppositis ovatis acutiusculis carnosis aveniis, umbellis petiolatis paucifloris (2–3) ebracteatis, floribus villoso-glandulosis, calycis tubo brevi brevi-subæqualiter 5-lobis, corollæ limbo valde obliquo longitudine tubi bilabiato coccineo flavo nigroque lineato, lobis subæqualibus ovatis, staminibus styloque corollæ longitudine.

For the introduction of living plants of this most lovely *Æschynanthus,* and for the opportunity of figuring it, we are indebted to Mr. Low, of the Clapton Nursery, who imported the species from Borneo. We are so fortunate as to possess dried specimens from the same country, gathered by Mr. Thomas Lobb. It is extremely different from any described *Æschynanthus,* and is well suited to ornament basket-work suspended to the roof in a moist stove. The branches droop considerably, and the flower-stalks, though the umbels are pendent, have an upward curvature, which adds considerably to the gracefulness and elegance of the species.

Descr. A smallish *plant,* at least flowering readily when of a small size; the *branches* rather long, disposed to climb or to hang down over the edge of a pot or basket, scandent naturally, and rooting from between the opposite leaves, terete, slightly downy. *Leaves* about an inch long, on short *petioles,* opposite,

February 1st, 1858.

exactly ovate, slightly acuminated but not sharp at the apex, a little downy, especially at the edge and beneath, quite entire. *Umbels* of few flowers, both axillary and terminal, solitary. *Peduncle* short, deflexed. *Pedicels* slender, and with an upward curvature, so that the flowers become erect. These are very beautiful and richly coloured. *Calyx* short, cup-shaped rather than tubular, red, the edge cut into five, erect, nearly equal, rounded *lobes*, villous with slender hairs tipped with minute glands. *Corolla* an inch and a half to two inches long, scarlet, streaked with bright-yellow and black, glanduloso-hirsute; tube rather short, curved, nearly thrice as long as the short calyx, gibbous on the anterior side; limb very oblique, about as long as the tube, bilabiate; upper lip of one, lower of three, ovate concave spreading segments. *Stamens* four, didynamous, meeting at the apex of the upper lip of the corolla, where the anthers combine. *Ovary* linear, cylindrical, downy, arising from the centre of a very large hemispherical, depressed gland. *Stigma* obscurely two-lipped.

Fig. 1. Ovary. 2. Calyx:—*magnified*.

W Fitch del et lith. Vincent Brooks Imp.

TAB. 5032.

CATTLEYA LUTEOLA.

Citron-coloured Cattleya.

Nat. Ord. ORCHIDEÆ.—GYNANDRIA MONANDRIA.

Gen. Char. (*Vide supra*, TAB. 4700.)

CATTLEYA *luteola;* parva, rhizomate repente ramoso, pseudobulbis fasciculat ovalibus oblongisve demum sulcatis, foliis solitariis oblongo-ellipticis carnoso-coriaceis crassis apice emarginatis, pedunculis vaginatis solitariis plurifloris, floribus parvis luteolis, ovario peduncuIiformi rectiusculo, sepalis petalisque conformibus patentibus oblongo-lanceolatis subflexuosis obtusis, labello perianthii longitudine trilobo intus velutino, lobis lateralibus elongatis incurvis columnam utrinque dentatam involventibus, intermedio rotundato crispato ciliato-denticulato.

CATTLEYA luteola. *Lindl. in Gard. Chron.* 1853, *p.* 774. *Reichenb. fil. Xenia, p.* 209. *t.* 83.

CATTLEYA modesta, *Meyer;* C. Meyeri, *Regel; and* C. flavida, *Klotzsch, according to Reichenbach fil.*

Received from the collection of Messrs. Rollison, Tooting Nursery, and I am indebted to Dr. Lindley for the above references and synonyms. As a species it is very unlike any with which I am acquainted. In colour it approaches the much more beautiful *Cattleya citrina*, but in scarcely any other character. It flowered with the Messrs. Rollison in November, 1857, and is known to be a native of Brazil.

DESCR. Our *plant* has an annulated branched *rhizome*, about as thick as a duck's quill, sending down from beneath a few thick fleshy fibres, and upwards, from the short branches, elliptical, quite smooth and compressed *pseudobulbs*, which bear one leaf, and while young are enveloped in a large, sheathed, membranous, striated, sheathing *scale*, these increase in age, and eventually become oblong, nearly terete and sulcated. *Leaf* about three inches long, thick, succulent, dark-green, elliptical, veinless, with a deep notch at the apex. From the base of this leaf, at the top of the pseudobulb, arises the *peduncle*, scarcely two inches long, enveloped entirely in a compressed membranaceous *sheath*, slit open on one side, four- or five- or more flowered. *Flowers* racemose, pale lemon-yellow, small for the genus. *Sepals* and *petals* uniform, an inch and a half to two inches at the most long, oblong-lanceolate, obtuse, a little waved, all spreading. *Lip* about as long as the segments of the perianth, three-lobed, velvety within, the side-lobes elongated, incurved, meeting over the column, and forming a kind of tube; the terminal lobe broad, almost orbicular, crisped and ciliato-dentate at the edge. *Column* much shorter than the lip, concealed within it, semiterete, with a wing or broad tooth at each margin above. *Anther-case* sunk into the clinandrium. *Pollen-masses* as in the genus, each pair with a short *cauda*.

Fig. 1. Lip. 2. Column. 3. Pollen-masses:—*magnified*.

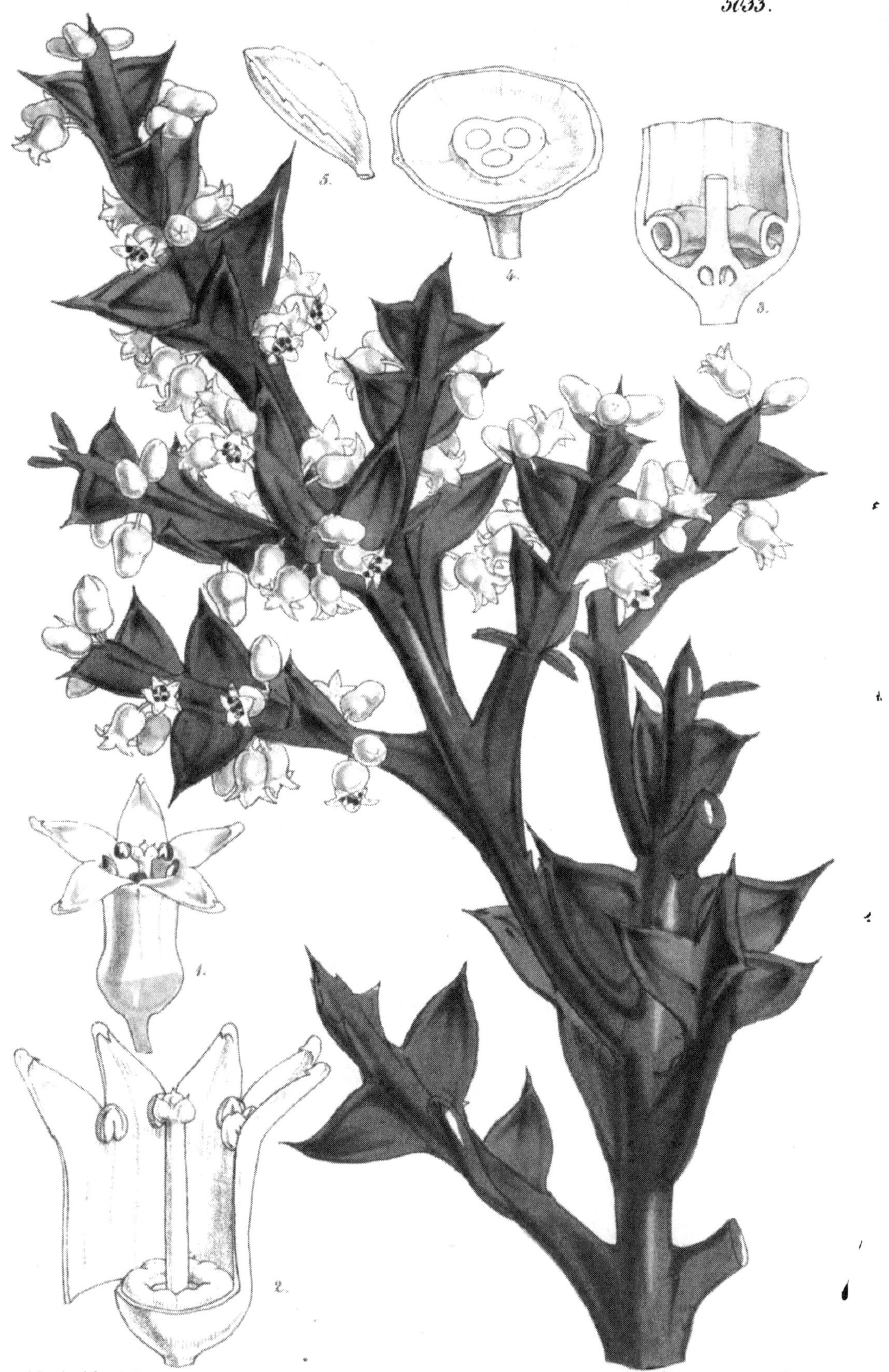

Fitch del et lith. Vincent Brooks Imp.

Tab. 5033.

COLLETIA CRUCIATA.

Cross-spined Colletia.

Nat. Ord. Rhamneæ.—Pentandria Monogynia.

Gen. Char. Calyx membranaceus, campanulatus v. tubulosus, limbi quinquefidi laciniis ovatis, suberectis; *disco* annulari, supra fundum tubi adnato, margine integro involuto. *Corolla* nulla. *Stamina* 5, inter lacinias calycis summo tubo rarius demissius inserta; *filamenta* filiformia, ad tubi fundum decurrentia. *Antheræ* reniformes, *loculis* apice confluentibus, uniloculares, hippocrepicæ, rima arcuata, bivalves. *Ovarium* liberum, globosum, triloculare. *Ovula* in loculis solitaria, e basi erecta, anatropa. *Stylus* filiformis, simplex, calycis tubum æquans. *Stigma* obsolete trilobum. *Fructus* siccus, sphæricus, calycis basi circumscissa libera vel inferne vix adhærente stipatus, trilocularis, tricoccus; *coccis* crustaceis, secedentibus, bivalvibus, monospermis. *Semina* erecta, ovata; *testa* crustacea, lævissima; *raphe* introrsum laterali. *Embryo* albuminis carnosi flavi strato tenui tectus, orthotropus; *cotyledonibus* maximis, carnosis, planis; *radicula* brevissima infera.—Suffrutices *Peruani et Chilenses, ramosissimi, subaphylli;* ramis *decussatim oppositis, divaricatis;* ramulis *spinescentibus, interdum foliaceo-dilatatis;* foliis *nullis v. minutissimis, oppositis, integerrimis;* floribus *axillaribus, fasciculatis v. infra spinarum basin sitis, nutantibus, albidis v. albido-roseis. Endl.*

Colletia *cruciata;* fruticosa, ramis viridibus cauleque spinis magnis ovato-triangularibus lateraliter compressis acutissimis horridis, foliis rarissimis minutis ellipticis deciduis, floribus lateralibus solitariis fasciculatisve.

Colletia cruciata. *Hook. et Arn. in Hook. Bot. Miscel.* 1830, *p.* 152.

Colletia Bictoniensis. *Lindl. in Journ. Hort. Soc. v.* 5. *p.* 31 *(with woodcut, excellent).*

"This, one of the most singular among the many curious plants in Dr. Gillies' rich collection from South America, was gathered during a hasty visit from his ship to the shores of the Banda Oriental, near Maldonado. It may be considered as a shrub whose stem and branches are constituted of a mass of opposite, decussated and decurrent, large, laterally compressed spines, of the same dull-green colour as the central portion that unites them, and equally woody; their tips are darker-coloured, sometimes brown, and very pungent. If the fascicle of flowers appears from any point except that of the base of a spine, it is either at the extremity or below some slight swelling, and is indicative of a new spine which is about to appear. The leaves are so rare, that upon the dried specimens only one could be found, and that upon one of the youngest branches. The form and structure of the flowers are very similar to those of *Colletia ferox*." Having thus published, twenty-eight years ago, my views of the general structure of this remarkable plant from native specimens, and alluded to no specific affinity with *C. spinosa* (also described in the same Memoir), it can hardly be expected I should concur in the extraordinary transformation represented to Dr. Lindley as having occurred at Bicton Park, Sidmouth, by the intelligent gardener to Lady Rolle, Mr. James Barnes, viz. in the rearing of *C. cruciata* from seed of *C. spinosa*. Let it be recollected, that "when Sir Philip Egerton first saw this plant at Bicton Gardens, and made inquiries of Mr. Barnes respecting it, the latter had quite forgotten its origin; but he had since a perfect recollection, and was reminded by the foreman of the Arboretum, that it was a seedling raised from *C. spinosa*." It is noways discreditable to Mr. Barnes to infer that the latter view may be erroneous, and that it is a plant which, through some channel or other, was directly received from the eastern (and not the western) side of South America, where I believe *C. spinosa* never occurs. It would require experiments of the most confirmed and satisfactory kind to show that this and *C. spinosa* (equally faithfully figured by Dr. Lindley, Journ. Hort. Soc. l. c. p. 30, woodcut) were one and the same species. We cultivate them both at Kew: one the Chilian species, *C. spinosa*, is perfectly hardy, and flowers without shelter; while our present plant will only succeed under the shelter of a wall, and never flowers. In Devonshire it is different. We have received the most beautiful specimens reared by Mr. Veitch, in Devonshire, and from these our figure is taken. The flowers, at first sight, much resemble those of some Ericaceous plant, and have quite a waxy appearance.

Descr. A *shrub* three to four feet high, copiously branched, the whole as it were made up of large, ovate-triangular, opposite and decussate, laterally compressed, green, yet woody, very pungent *spines*, singularly decurrent at the base. Here and there, chiefly on the younger branches or small terminal spines, an opposite pair of minute, elliptical, serrated *leaves* are to be seen; but these soon fall away. From the base of the spines the *flowers* appear on short *peduncles*, solitary or fasciculate, two to four from the same point, drooping, yellowish-white, tinged with green at the base. *Perianth* single (calyx), the tube cylindrical, but a little swollen at the base, where there is a little difference in texture, which difference terminates where the curious annulus is situated, and which is characteristic of the genus *Colletia*; this forms a ring within, above the base of the perianth, is fleshy, and singularly involute; *limb* of five, narrow ovate segments, hooked at the points. The *ovary* is small, half sunk into the base of the perianth, three-celled, each cell with one ovule. *Style* terete, as long as the tube of the perianth. *Stigma* three-lobed.

Fig. 1. Flower. 2. Flower laid open to show the interior, the annulus, style, and stamens. 3. Base of the flower cut through vertically. 4. Base of the disc. 5, 6. Leaf:—*magnified.*

5034.

Tab. 5034.

GAULTHERIA discolor.

Two-coloured Gaultheria.

Nat. Ord. Ericeæ.—Decandria Monogynia.

Gen. Char. *Calyx* quinquelobus, demum ampliatus, plus minus baccatus et capsulam ambiens aut fovens. *Corolla* ovata, ore sæpe contracta, 5-dentata. *Stamina* 10, inclusa; *filamentis* sæpe villosis; *antheris* 4-aristatis, nempe apice bifidis, loculis biaristatis rarissime muticis. *Stylus* filiformis. *Stigma* obtusum. *Squamæ hypogynæ* 10, distinctæ aut concretæ. *Capsula* depresso-globosa, 5-locularis, 5-sulcatis, 5-valvis; *valvis* septiferis, loculicidis, dehiscentibus. *Placentæ* axi adnatæ. *Semina* plurima, parva, testa subreticulata.—Frutices *aut rarius* arbusculæ, *ex* America, *rarius ex* India, *orti.* Folia *alterna, sempervirentia, dentata aut integerrima.* Pedicelli *nunc axillares,* 1-*flori, nunc in racemum terminalem dispositi, bibracteolati.* Corollæ *albæ roseæ aut coccineæ. De Cand.*

Gaultheria *discolor;* ramulis glabratis, foliis obovato-lanceolatis acuminatis subserratis subtus argenteis, nervis paucis margine subparallelis, racemis brevibus 6–8-floris, pedicellis ciliatis bracteolatis, bracteolis parvis oblongis acutis, sepalis ovatis acutis ciliolatis, corollæ fauce barbata, lobis roseis, filamentis setulosis, antheris apice bicuspidatis, ovario villoso, disco 10-dentato.

Gaultheria discolor. *Nuttall, MSS.*

A very elegant little species, discovered in the temperate regions of the Bhotan Himalaya by Mr. Booth, and raised by our indefatigable friend Mr. Nuttall, of Nutgrove, near Rainhill, Lancashire. Its nearest ally is the common Himalayan *G. fragrantissima,* from which, as from all its allies, the beautiful silvery under surface of the leaves at once distinguishes it.

A small, almost glabrous, *shrub*. *Branches* rather slender, angled. *Leaves* about an inch long, shortly petioled, obovate-lanceolate, remotely and sharply but not deeply serrate, acuminate, narrowed at the base, dark-green above, silvery-white beneath. *Nerves* few, springing from near the base of the midrib and running nearly parallel to the margin of the leaf. *Racemes* short, axillary, few-flowered, much shorter than the leaves. *Flowers* small, crowded, shortly pedicelled, about one-third of an inch long. *Calyx*, bracteoles and pedicels white. *Corolla* white, with bright-pink lobes, hairy at the mouth and base of the lobes. *Filaments* ciliated with stiff setæ. *Anther-lobes* mucronate at the tip. *Ovary* villous.

Fig. 1. Flower, pedicels, and bracts. 2. Stamen. 3. Pistil. 4. Immature fruit:—*all magnified.*

W. Fitch del. et lith. Vincent Brooks Imp.

TAB. 5035.

PILUMNA FRAGRANS.

Fragant Pilumna.

Nat. Ord. ORCHIDEÆ.—GYNANDRIA MONANDRIA.

Gen. Char. Ovarium tricostatum. *Sepala* et *petala* æqualia, patula, oblique inserta. *Labellum* basi columnæ adnatum, subintegrum, orbiculatum, convolutum, inappendiculatum. *Columna* clavata, teres. *Clinandrium* cucullo dentato membranaceo circumdatum; furcis duabus carnosis semiclausum. *Stigma* verticale. *Pollinia* 2, postice fissa, caudiculæ brevi et glandulæ ovatæ adnata.—Herbæ *epiphytæ;* pseudobulbis *vaginatis;* foliis *coriaceis;* pedunculis *radicalibus.* —Genus *Aspasiæ* proximum, clinandrio cucullato, columna tereti, necnon stigmate verticali nec fasciali diversum. *Lindl.*

PILUMNA *fragrans;* folio lato oblongo racemo 2–3-floro breviore, bracteis lanceolatis erectis obtusis, sepalis petalisque oblongo-lanceolatis acuminatis, labello oblongo apiculato subtrilobo lævi. *Lindl.*

PILUMNA fragrans. *Lindl. Bot. Reg.* 1844, *Misc. p.* 74. *n.*

TRICHOPILIA albida. *Wendl. fil. in Regel's Gartenflora*, 1854, *p.* 43. *t.* 78.

For this charming and deliciously scented plant the Royal Gardens are indebted to Lady Dorothy Nevill, whose good taste and love of horticulture, combined with those of Mr. Nevill, have made Dangstein already the site of one of the best private gardens in England. The plant is said to be a native of Popayan, and discovered by Hartweg, though this has been considered (as Dr. Lindley says the *P. laxa* was stated to be, but he suspected erroneously) purchased at one of Mr. Skinner's sales of Guatemala plants. It has borne in some gardens the name of *Trichopilia albida*, and such a plant is indeed figured on a reduced scale by M. Regel in his 'Gartenflora' above quoted. Our plant, we cannot doubt, is the *Pilumna fragrans.* The only other species of this genus yet known, is the *P. laxa*, Lindl. Bot. Reg. 1846, t. 57, which has much smaller and differently coloured flowers, wanting the orange spot in the labellum, and has a very differently formed pseudobulb. The plant flowered in great perfection in December, 1857.

DESCR. *Pseudobulb* oblong, four to six inches long, subterete or slightly compressed, smooth, monophyllous, sheathed at the base with three or four large faintly striated membranaceous *scales*. *Leaf* oblong-lanceolate, six to eight inches long, acute, smooth, veinless, rather fleshy and opaque. *Peduncle* arising from the base of the pseudobulb, pendent, about a foot long, including the *flowers:* these are large, handsome, four or more in a bracteated *raceme*. *Bracteas* ovato-oblong, acute, withering. *Pedicels* two inches long, but gradually passing into the club-shaped, three-furrowed ovary. *Sepals* and *petals* nearly uniform, long (two and a half to three inches), very much spreading, linear-lanceolate, acuminate, slightly twisted. *Lip* very large, the lower part of the *claw* united to the column; the rest involute, so as to enclose the column; from the claw the *limb* suddenly expands so as to be very large, almost orbicular, obscurely three-lobed, pure white, with an orange spot at its base on the disc. *Column* terete and club-shaped. *Clinandrium* with two rounded entire ears in front, at the back three-lobed and fimbriated. *Anther-case* operculiform. *Pollen-masses* two, with a caudicle and linear *gland*.

Fig. 1. Column. 2. Pollen-masses:—*magnified*.

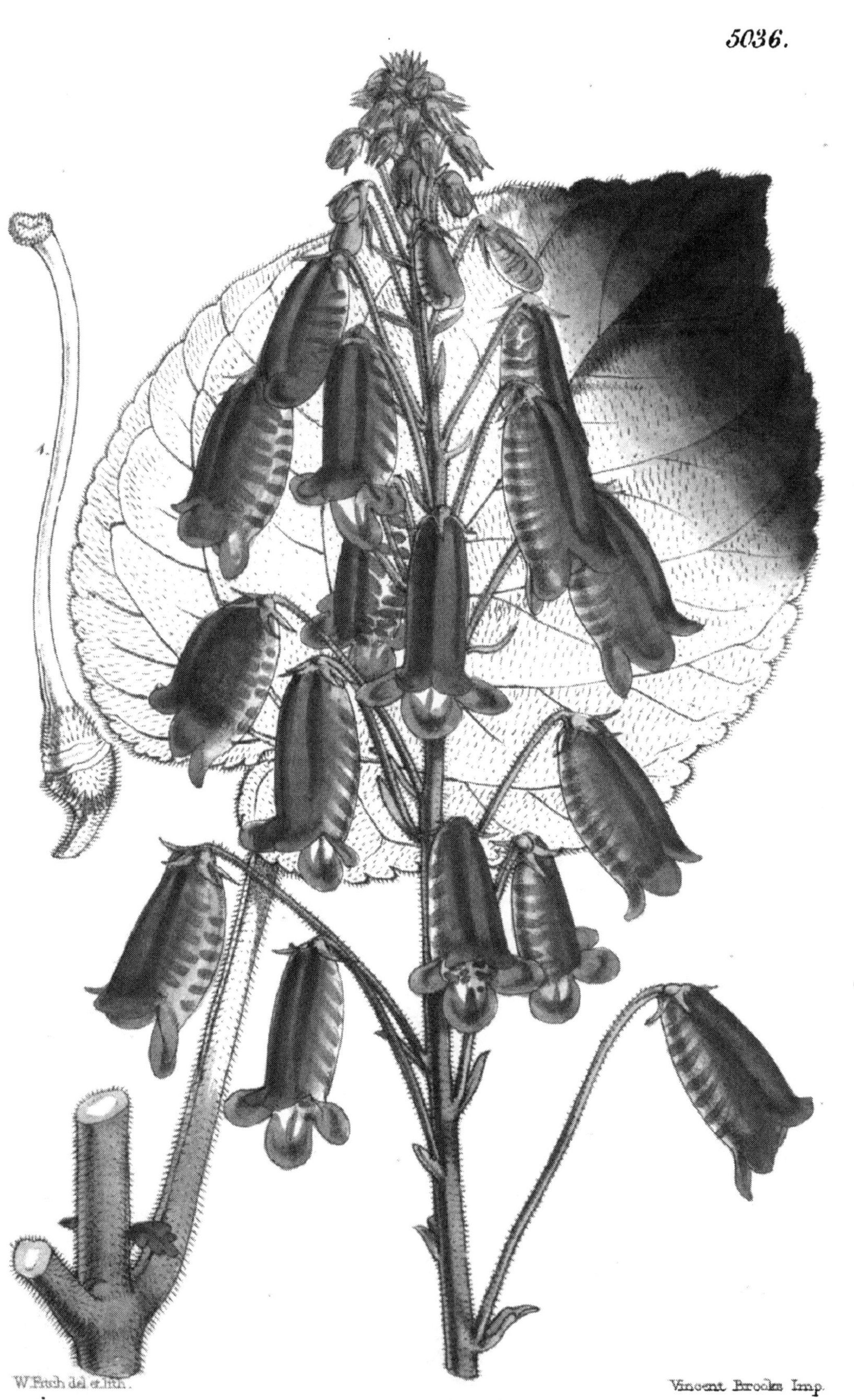
5036.
1.
W. Fitch del. et lith.
Vincent Brooks Imp.

Tab. 5036.

GESNERIA cinnabarina.

Cinnabar-flowered Gesneria.

Nat. Ord. Gesneriaceæ.—Didynamia Angiospermia.

Gen. Char. (*Vide supra*, Tab. 4217.)

Gesneria (§ Nægelia) *cinnabarina;* tota molliter glanduloso-pubescens, caule erecto, foliis cordato-rotundatis duplicato-crenatis purpureo-variegatis, panicula terminali elongata multiflora, bracteis linearibus oblongisve integris lobatisve, pedicellis elongatis, calycis parvi lobis lato-subulatis patentibus, corolla rubra subtus albo-fasciata usque ad basin ventricosa, limbi lobis brevibus rotundatis, labio inferiore patente, ovario patente, disco annulari subintegro.

Nægelia cinnabarina. *Linden, Suppl. de Cat. des Pl. Exot. du Jard. de Brux.* 1856 (*figure only, unaccompanied by description.*)

The *Gesneriaceæ* of the Royal Garden and Herbarium of Berlin alone, have furnished to Dr. Hansteen materials for a memoir on the family, which he divides into 2 tribes, 12 sub-tribes, and 68 genera: how far it might be desirable to consider many of these 68 sections as sub-genera rather than genera, I am not in a position to say. The present plant, together with the well-known *Gesneria zebrina*, would fall into his genus *Nægelia* of his tribe 1, *Gesnereæ*, and 3rd sub-tribe, *Brachylomateæ*, and is distinguished by "Corolla oblique adnata, tubo ventre inflato, dorso recto, limbo inæqualiter quinquelobo, fauce late hiante. Annulus perigynus quinquecrenatus. Stigma capitatum. Reliqua ut in Gesneria." So very much does the present species resemble the well-known *Gesneria zebrina* (figured by us at Tab. 3940), that it might easily be passed by as a variety of that plant, and in habit, size, pubescence (soft and velvety), shape of the leaves, and inflorescence, that our full description given under that Tab., may well enable us to dispense with a repetition here. The sole difference is the flowers: yet even these are liable to some variation. The calyx here has acuminated almost subulate lobes, which spread horizontally (not short and erect). The corolla, though about the same size, is different in colour, being of a brick-red, paler beneath, and there banded with white; the ventricose character is extended to the very base of the corolla, wanting the contraction at the base of the tube, so conspicuous in *G. zebrina*. The limb is less oblique, the lower lip less porrected, more patent. In the figure of Linden, the upper part of the tube exhibits more yellow than in our plant, and that is a nearer approach to the *G. zebrina;* and the lobes are more acute. It is described as a native of the forests of Chiapas, a State of the Mexican Confederation which formerly belonged to Guatemala, where it was discovered by Ghiesbrecht.

Fig. 1. Pistil, *magnified.*

5037.

Tab. 5037.

DENDROBIUM pulchellum.

Showy Dendrobium.

Nat. Ord. Orchideæ.—Gynandria Monandria.

Gen. Char. (*Vide supra*, Tab. 4755.)

Dendrobium *pulchellum;* caulibus teretibus striatis pendulis, foliis oblongo-lanceolatis subplicatis, pedunculis unifloris (racemis lateralibus strictis multifloris, Roxb.), bracteis brevibus ovatis obtusis, sepalis patentibus oblongis apiculatis, petalis patentibus sepalis triplo majoribus ovalibus obtusis striatis, labello basi obtuso breviter calcarato unguiculato cochleariformi striato villoso pulcherrime fimbriato-ciliato, ungue lobis 2-involutis.

Dendrobium pulchellum. *Roxb. Fl. Indica, v.* 3. *p.* 486? *Lindl. Gen. et. Sp. Orchid. p.* 82? *Hensl. in Maund's Botanist, v.* 1. *t.* 5. *Loddiges, Bot. Cab. t.* 1935.

That this is the *Dendrobium pulchellum* of our gardens, and of Maund and Loddiges, there can be no manner of doubt, but I am by no means clear about it being the *D. pulchellum* of Roxburgh and Lindley. Dr. Lindley first published the plant, as it would appear, from the 'Icones Pictæ' and MSS. of Dr. Roxburgh in the possession of the Honourable the India Company, but he describes the "*racemes* lateral, strict, and many-flowered." Roxburgh, in the last volume of the 'Flora Indica,' does the same, as we understand his words: "Raceme lateral," in the specific character; and in the description, "Racemes lateral, from the old leafless stems or branches, diverging, flexuose, with one large pale pink flower at each of the six or eight curvatures." Now this is totally at variance with the inflorescence of our plant, and with the *figures* in Maund and in Loddiges: notwithstanding which the specific character and description, in Maund, make the flowers to be in "many-flowered racemes." Loddiges, more prudently, gives neither character nor description. Lindley again, probably deriving his information from Roxburgh's drawing, says: "Sepala alba; petala rosea; labellum lutescens, macula basi rubro-aurantiaca;" which hardly accords with the flowers of the *Dendrobium* before us. Our plant, therefore, we wish to be considered the *D. pulchellum* of the gardens; doubtfully of Roxburgh and Lindley. If the plant of these latter authors, it is a native of the rocks and trees in the forest of the Silhet hills," according to Roxburgh.

Descr. Our *plants* are small, epiphytal. *Stems*, or leafy *pseudobulbs*, growing several from one point, more or less pendent, striated, scarcely a span long, subterete, jointed, throwing out *radicles* from different points. *Leaves* alternate, scarcely two inches long, oblong, acute, fleshy, patent, sheathing the stem at the base. *Flowers*, in our specimen solitary from the joints of the stem, generally from those portions where the leaves have fallen. *Pedicels* short, gradually passing into the clavate inferior ovary, with small appressed *bracts* at the base. *Sepals* spreading, equal, oblong, subacute, faintly striated, pale purple. *Petals* much larger than the sepals, oval, obtuse, striated, purple-lilac. *Labellum* large, orbicular, concave, villous, beautifully and finely fringed at the margin; clawed at the base, and the claw bears two incurved small lobes: colour of the lip purple at the edge; the *disc* orange, white between the orange disc and the purple margin.

Fig. 1. Column. 2. Pollen-masses. 3. Labellum:—*magnified*.

W Fitch del et Lith.

Vincent Brooks Imp.

Tab. 5038

HYDRANGEA cyanema.

Blue-stamened Hydrangea.

Nat. Ord. Saxifragaceæ: Tribe Hydrangeæ.—Decandria Trigynia.

Gen. Char. (*Vide supra*, Tab. 4253.)

Hydrangea *cyanema;* ramulis corymbosis petiolisque pubescentibus, foliis late ovatis grosse serrato-dentatis utrinque pubescentibus margine ciliatis, fl. imperfect. sepalis 3–5 albis cuneato-ovatis grosse sinuato-crenatis, stylis 3–5 liberis brevibus.

Hydrangea cyanema. *Nutt. MSS.*

One of the many interesting Himalayan plants introduced by Mr. Nuttall from Bhotan, where it was discovered by Mr. Booth. As a species it is exactly intermediate in characters between the *H. robusta*, H.f. and T., and *H. stylosa*, H.f. and T., both natives of the adjoining province of Sikkim. It is indeed possible that *H. cyanema* may prove to be a variety of one of these, for the arborescent species of *Hydrangea* (amongst which this no doubt will rank) are with difficulty recognized in a young state, and some of the most distinctive marks of the species reside in the capsules, which are in this plant not formed. *H. stylosa*, with which *H. cyanema* accords perfectly in habit, foliage, and the sepals of the imperfect flowers, differs in having very slender subulate styles; and *H. robusta*, with which Mr. Nuttall's plant agrees in the colour of the peduncles, pedicels, calyx, stamens, etc., and in the form of the styles, is a very robust species, with broader, usually cordate leaves, deeply and closely toothed and fimbriated, and the petiole is generally winged, and the sepals of the imperfect flowers are acutely toothed.

Descr. *Stem* apparently subscandent (as in young individuals of various species), pubescent, as are the leaves on both surfaces and inflorescence. *Leaves* shortly petioled, ovate, acute, coarsely serrato-dentate, ciliated; *petiole* not winged. *Corymb* spreading, rather loose; *pedicels* red. *Imperfect flowers* with three to five broadly-ovate or obcuneate, sessile, white, sinuate, toothed *sepals,* faintly veined with red-purple. *Perfect flowers* small, scattered, glabrous. *Petals* and *stamens* blue. *Ovary* with three robust, recurved *styles,* which are free to the base.

Fig. 1. Imperfect flower, from which the sepals have been cut away. 2. Perfect flower. 3. Calyx and pistil:—*magnified.*

W Fitch del. et lith.

Vincent Brooks Imp.

Tab. 5039.

CATTLEYA Aclandiæ.

Lady Acland's Cattleya.

Nat. Ord. Orchideæ.—Gynandria Monandria.

Gen. Char. (*Vide supra,* Tab. 4700.)

Cattleya *Aclandiæ;* foliis ellipticis, floribus binis, sepalis petalisque herbaceis obovato-lanceolatis æqualibus undulatis purpureo-maculatis, labelli plani calvi hypochilio dilatato paulo subrepando epichilio orbiculari reniformi emarginato. *Lindl.*

Cattleya Aclandiæ. *Lindl. Bot. Reg. v.* 26. *t.* 48. *Paxt. Mag. of Bot. v.* 9. *t.* 1. *Fl. des Serres, v.* 7. *t.* 674.

One of the handsomest of a very handsome genus, distinguished by Dr. Lindley with the name of the late lamented Lady Acland, of Killerton, Devon, by whom the plant was first introduced from Brazil, and from a drawing by her Ladyship the figure in the 'Botanical Register' was engraved. We have since received living plants from Bahia through our obliging friend J. Wetherall, now her B. M. Consul at Paraiba, Brazil. The flowers are charmingly varied in colour, and the structure of the labellum departs from the usual form, constituting (with *Cattleya bicolor*) a distinct section of the genus, distinguished by the base of the lip being too narrow and too spreading to cover the column. With us, April has been its flowering season in a warm stove.

Descr. *Pseudobulbs* cauliform, terete, jointed, four to five inches long, striated, branched at the base, and sheathed with membranaceous *spathes* at the joints. *Leaves* two, terminal, elliptical, obtuse, thick and fleshy. From the centre of this pair of leaves the peduncle appears, bearing two large very handsome *flowers*. *Sepals* and *petals* uniform, spreading, two to two and a quarter inches long, obovato-lanceolate, firm, fleshy, yellow-green, strongly spotted and blotched with dark purple on the upper or anterior side, much less distinctly so at the back. *Lip* large, porrected, much larger than the petals or sepals, panduriform;

March 1st, 1858.

the base narrow and spreading, with two lateral lobes so small that they do not include the column, as is usual in this genus; the lip is still more contracted near the middle, whence it expands into the broad, kidney-shaped extremity, emarginate at the apex: the colour of the whole is pale purple, with darker veins, and a yellow line on the disc. *Column* parallel with the lip, and, as it were, applied to it, obovate, dark-purple, expanding into two wing-like margins. *Anther-case* sunk between two teeth or small lobes of the *clinandrium*. *Pollen-masses* as in the genus.

Fig. 1. Column. 2. Pollen-masses. 3. Lip:—*all more or less magnified.*

5040.

W. Fitch del. et lith.   Vincent Brooks Imp.

Tab. 5040.

EUGENIA Luma.

Pointed-leaved Eugenia.

Nat. Ord. Myrtaceæ.—Icosandria Monogynia.

Gen. Char. Calycis tubus subglobosus, supra germen haud v. vix productus. *Germen* inferum, 2–3-loculare, multiovulatum; *ovula* sporophoris centralibus affixa. *Sepala* 4, subrotunda, brevia, rarissime ovata v. acuta. *Petala* 4, margini tubi calycis inserta. *Stamina* plurima, cum petalis inserta, perigyna, libera, in alabastro incurvata; *antheræ* biloculares, longitudinaliter dehiscentes. *Stylus* solitarius; *stigma* simplex. *Fructus* baccatus v. drupaceus, tunc pyrenis cartilagineis donatus, *disco* plano calyceque coronatus, 1–4-spermus. *Embryo* exalbuminosus, carnosus; *cotyledonibus* sæpissime margine v. omnino conferruminatis; *radicula* abbreviata. *Berg, in Linnæa, v.* 27.

Eugenia *Luma;* ramulis foliisque novellis ad petiolum costam medium et marginem pedunculisque puberulis, foliis petiolatis rigide coriaceis ovalibus v. ovali-oblongis cuspidato-acuminatis basi acutis adultis glabris vix punctatis supra aveniis subtus pallidioribus venosis limbinerviis, pedunculis axillaribus folio longioribus 1–2-nis aut omnibus 3–5-floris aut altero unifloro altero trifloro aut summis omnino unifloris, germine biloculari, sepalis subrotundis ciliolatis glabris. *Berg.*

Engenia Luma. *Berg. in Linnæa, v.* 27. *p.* 251.

Eugenia apiculata. *De Cand. Prodr. v.* 3. *p.* 273. *Hook. et Arn. Bot. Misc. v.* 3. *p.* 321. *Cl. Gay, Fl. Chil. v.* 2. *p.* 398.

Myrtus Luma. *Molina Chil. v.* 2. *p.* 289.

A charming shrub, from the open border of the nursery of Messrs. Veitch and Sons, who introduced the species from Chili, through Mr. Wm. Lobb. It is quite equal in beauty to our common Myrtle, and no more need be said to recommend it as an ornamental evergreen shrub for our gardens. It blossoms in the summer months, when the branches are literally loaded with the white blossoms, almost concealing the copious foliage; the leaves indeed are not much unlike those of the common Myrtle, but broader and suddenly and sharply apiculated. It inhabits the colder parts of Chili, from Concepcion to the island of Chiloe,

March 1st, 1858.

and Valdivia, and hence its hardiness may be accounted for. It is called "*Arroyan*" by the natives.

Descr. A *shrub*, varying, it is said, much in size in its native country, from three to several feet in height, copiously branched; *branchlets*, *petioles*, and *veins* beneath ferruginously downy. *Leaves* copious, opposite, nearly sessile, about three-fourths of an inch long, broad, oval, approaching to orbicular, but acute at the base and sharply apiculate at the point; above, in the living state, distinctly pinnately veined, indistinctly so when dry; beneath paler and more obovately veined and reticulated, obscurely dotted, and having a marginal vein. *Flowers* solitary, on rather short *peduncles*, or the *peduncles* are branched and bear from three to five moderately large white *flowers*. These also a good deal resemble the common Myrtle, but the *petals* are larger and more concave. There is a pair of *bracts* at the base of the ovary. *Stamens* numerous. *Petals* four. *Ovary* two-celled. *Cells* two-seeded.

Fig. 1. Two flower-buds and expanded flower, from which the stamens and petals are removed. 2. Transverse section of ovary:—*magnified*.

5041.

W Fitch del et lith.

Vincent Brooks Imp.

Tab. 5041.

DASYLIRIUM glaucophyllum.

Glaucous-leaved Dasylirium.

Nat. Ord. Asparagineæ.—Diœcia Hexandria.

Gen. Char. (*Vide supra*, Tab. 5030.)

Dasylirium *glaucophyllum*; caulescens, foliis longissimis e lata basi lineari-subulatis insigniter glaucis apicibus integris (fasciculo fibrarum emarcidarum *non* terminatis) planiusculis striatis marginatis rigide serrulatis spinosisque, spinis subulatis sursum curvatis, spica longissima composita, spiculis seu racemis cylindricis copiosis dense compactis multifloris, bracteis e lata basi subulatis, floribus dense imbricatis masculorum filamentis longe exsertis.

Plants of this species of *Dasylirium* were received at the Royal Gardens of Kew at the same time with the *D. acrotrichum*, and from the same source, namely, from Mr. Repper, of Real del Monte; and the same unusually warm summer which encouraged the blossoming of that species, no doubt had its influence on this, and it came to perfection at the same time. The flowering stem was about eleven feet high; probably, as the plants increase in size, the flower-stem will also be larger. I regret that I cannot find this anywhere described, yet it has well-marked characters in the very glaucous hue of the more strict and rigid (not gracefully drooping) leaves, and in the integrity of the apices of the leaves, which do not break out in the tufts or pencils of strong fibres as they do in *D. acrotrichum*.

Descr. The *stem* of our plant, though of an arborescent character, is not more than a foot high, thicker than a man's arm, scarred with the marks of fallen leaves, and crowned at the top with a tuft of beautiful foliage. *Leaves* three feet and more long, spreading in all directions, but not recurved, rigid, strict, from a broad base linear-subulate, tapering gradually into a fine *entire* point, that is, it does *not* break up at the apex into a pencil or tuft of rigid tough fibres; striated, margined with a narrow cartilaginous edge, which is minutely serrated, and rather distantly beset with small, subulate, falcate, very sharp *spines*.

From the centre of the stem arises the *peduncle*, which, including the long spike, rises ten to twelve feet: upon this *peduncle*, which is stout in proportion to its height, the leaves gradually pass into subulate *bracts*, which become as though one higher up in the compound *spike*. MALE PLANT: *Spike* yellow. *Flowers* very dense on the spikelets, small, each of six, obovate, retuse, erect *sepals*, greenish-white, streaked with red at the tip. *Stamens* six, large. *Filaments* much exserted. *Anthers* oblong, yellow, large. *Abortive ovary* three, small, conical bulbs on the disc.—A few of the flowers proved to be female: *ovary* obcordate, three-lobed, abortive in our plant.

Fig. 1. Plant, *greatly reduced in size*. 2. Apex of a leaf, *nat. size*. 3. Upper portion of a male spike, *nat. size*. 4. Portion of a leaf. 5. Male flower. 6. Abortive pistil. 7. Ovary from a female flower:—*magnified*.

5042.

W. Fitch del. et lith. Vincent Brooks Imp.

TAB. 5042.

CALANTHE DOMINII (HYBRIDA).

Hybrid Calanthe.

Nat. Ord. ORCHIDEÆ.—GYNANDRIA MONANDRIA.

Gen. Char. *Perianthium* explanatum, liberum v. sepalis lateralibus labello paululum adnatis, subæquale. *Labellum* cum columna connatum, lobatum v. integrum, calcaratum v. muticum, disco lamellatum v. tuberculatum. *Columna* brevis, rostello sæpius rostrato. *Pollinia* 8, basi valde attenuata, quaternatim glandulæ bipartibili adhærentia.—*Terrestres*, scapis *erectis multifloris*. Folia *lata, plicata*. Flores *albi aut lilacini, raro lutei*. *Lindl.*

CALANTHE *Dominii;* hybrid between *C. furcata* and *C. Masuca.*

CALANTHE Dominii. *Lindl. in Gard. Chron.* 1858. *p.* 4.

Calanthe Masuca, Lindl., a purple-flowered species, is figured at our Tab. 4541. *Calanthe furcata* is a species described by Mr. Bateman (Bot. Reg. 1838, Misc. 34), chiefly differing from *C. veratrifolia* (a white-flowered kind, see our figure, Tab. 2615) in the larger size of the lateral lobes of the lip. Of the plant now under consideration, which was reared in the Exotic Nursery of Mr. James Veitch, jun., King's Road, Chelsea, and exhibited to Dr. Lindley, that gentleman remarks: "One might have said that the flowers were just intermediate (between the two now mentioned) in all respects. He would have considered it either as a purple-flowered *C. furcata*, or as a fork-spurred, small-flowered *C. Masuca.* Had hybrids been suspected to occur among Orchids, the plant would have been pronounced a cross,—and such it was." It is on this account that we figure so interesting a plant here, and for the sake of introducing Dr. Lindley's further remarks upon it, and of securing to Mr. Dominy the right of priority in the difficult operation of rearing hybrid Orchids.

"It appears that it had been raised in the Exeter Nursery by Mr. Dominy, Messrs. Veitch's indefatigable and very intelligent foreman, between *C. Masuca* and *C. furcata*. The seed was obtained in 1854 by crossing those two species, was immediately sown, *and in two years the seedlings were in flower*. Nor is it the least remarkable circumstance connected with this production, that it grows and flowers freely, while *C. Masuca* is a shy plant. We therefore propose, with much pleasure, that the name of the hybrid be *Calanthe Dominii,* in order to put upon permanent record the name of the first man who succeeded in this operation. He is indeed especially entitled to this distinction, not only in consequence of having produced other Orchidaceous mules, among which we understand our Cattleyas, but because of his eminent success in raising such plants from seed, as a matter of horticultural business.

"It is by no means our intention, in making the last remark, to claim for Mr. Dominy the merit of being the first gardener to raise seedling Orchids. On the contrary, about the year 1822, *Prescotia plantaginea* was raised abundantly in the garden of the Horticultural Society; and it has been rumoured for some time that seedling epiphytes are coming forward in certain Continental nurseries. What we do claim for him is therefore the priority in raising *hybrid* Orchids, a claim which will hardly be contested."—*Lindl. in Gard. Chron.*

Fig. 1. Lip and portion of the spur. 2. Pollen-masses :—*magnified*.

5043.

W Fitch del et lith.

Vincent Brooks Imp

Tab. 5043.

NIPHÆA albo-lineata; var. *reticulata.*

White-lined Niphæa; reticulated var.

Nat. Ord. Gesneriaceæ.—Didynamia Angiospermia.

Gen. Char. Calyx semisuperus, æqualis, 5-partitus. *Corolla* rotata, subæqualis; laciniis superioribus paulo minoribus et magis connatis. *Stamina* inclusa, libera, conniventia; 4 fertilia subæqualia, *antheris* glabris ovatis; quintum sterile, carnosum, *corollæ* dorso suo adnatum, deforme. *Glandulæ perigynæ* 0. *Ovarium* uniloculare, placentis didymis polyspermis. *Stigma* simplex.—Herbæ Ramondiæ *cujusdam caulescentis facie; foliis rugosis in verticillum approximatis; floribus axillaribus terminalibusque aggregatis, candidis. Lindl.*

Niphæa *albo-lineata;* hirsuta, foliis oppositis lineis albis pictis, internodiis elongatis, segmentis calycinis rotundatis tuboque hispidis.

Niphæa albo-lineata. *Hook. Bot. Mag. t.* 4282. *Hanstein in Linnæa, v.* 27. *p.* 704.

Var. *reticulata;* foliis remotis albo-reticulatis, pedunculis in axillis pluribus quasi verticillatis. (Tab. Nostr. 5043.)

The original species of *Niphæa*, as figured and described by Dr. Lindley, l.c., had the few pairs of leaves so approximate as to appear whorled in fours on the upper part of the stem, and the peduncles seemed to arise from the apex of the plant; in short, were terminal. In our *N. albo-lineata*, given at Tab. 4282, the pairs of leaves are rather remote, but the upper ones are so far crowded as still to appear to be all terminal; in our present plant, which we take to be a variety of, but larger and handsomer than that species, the pairs of leaves are still more remote, and the peduncles show themselves to be in whorls, or rather pseudo-whorls, from the axils of the distant pairs of leaves. This may be the effect of cultivation, but the character of the plant is thereby improved. The variegated foliage is as conspicuous here as in the original *albo-lineata*, but the lines anastomose so as to be at least partially reticulated. Hanstein has made a variety of *N. albo-lineata*, which he calls β *reticulata*, "nervis omnibus albo-reticulata;" and to this he refers the *N. argyroneura* of

April 1st, 1858.

Planchon and Linden, "Fl. des Serres, 8. 823. p. 201," and also *N. anœchtochilifolia* of Warsz. MSS., under which name we received our plant from Berlin. Indeed, except the variegated leaves and smaller flowers, there is scarcely any tangible specific difference between the two. The humbler growth of the original species, giving it a good deal the appearance of *Ramondia*, as the author correctly observes, was due probably to imperfect cultivation.

Fig. 1. Corolla laid open. 2. Pistil; the greater part of the ovary incorporated with the very hispid calyx-tube:—*magnified.*

5044.
1.
W. Fitch del et lith.
Vincent Brooks Imp.

Tab. 5044.

CAMELLIA rosæflora.

Rose-flowered Camellia.

Nat. Ord. Ternstrœmiaceæ.—Monadelphia Polyandria.

Gen. Char. (*Vide supra*, Tab. 2745.)

Camellia *rosæflora;* ramis patentibus glabris, foliis ovatis acuminatis argute serratis subcoriaceis glabris, floribus axillaribus solitariis declinatis, pedunculis brevissimis bracteatis, petalis obcordato-emarginatis, ovario styloque glaberrimis, stigmatibus elongatis.

This really handsome *Camellia* has been long cultivated in the Royal Gardens of Kew under the incorrect name of "*Camellia euryoides*, Lindl.," a very peculiar species, first figured and described by Dr. Lindley: the history of which is, that it was "a *stock* on which the Chinese graft their varieties of *Camellia Japonica*. The grafted portion of a *Camellia* brought from China for the Horticultural Society by Potts, in 1822, having died, the stock sprang up and produced this plant. The same having again befallen a *Camellia* brought home for the Society in 1824, by Mr. J. D. Parks, this plant again shot forth." Strange to say, nothing further is known of the original *C. euryoides*, and no systematic botanist, that I am aware of, has ever further noticed it. Our present plant, of which I know not the history, is quite different from this, more robust in habit, glabrous even in the young shoots, much larger in the flowers, which are pink-coloured. In some respects this approaches the *C. assimilis*, Champ., in Hook. Kew Gard. Misc. v. 3. p. 310, and Seemann, Bot. of H.M.S. Herald; but there the flowers are solitary and *terminal*, the stigma is small and obscurely three-lobed, the pistil very hairy, as are all the free filaments of the stamens.

Descr. Our plant is a *shrub*, three feet high, with a much more lax and straggling habit than that of the common *Camellia Japonica*. *Branches* rather twiggy, patent, clothed with a brown, quite smooth bark. *Leaves* ovate, acuminate, shortly petiolate, firm, subcoriaceous, dark glossy-green, strongly serrated at the margin, the base and acumen entire, rarely plane, slightly convex above, a little waved, the apex obtuse. *Flowers* axillary, solitary or rarely two together, opening in succession from the upper ones downwards, sessile or nearly so, appearing more decidedly sessile from the fact of the short *peduncle* being clothed with imbricated *scales*, white or a little silky at the back, small, at the base oval, gradually enlarging upwards till they pass into the imbricated lobes of the calyx. *Flowers* much larger than those of *C. Sasangua,* and much smaller than the ordinary size of *C. Japonica.* *Petals* generally six, of a clear, full pink or rose-colour, obcordate, but tapering so as to be cuneate at the base, and there slightly united in two series, imbricated, never fully patent, almost forming a tube below; the upper part more or less patent, the apex retuse or emarginate. *Stamens* not very numerous (twenty-five to thirty); *filaments* united in their lower half into a firm, fleshy *tube.* *Anthers* small, yellow. *Ovary* subglobose, quite glabrous. *Style* nearly as long as the stamens, stout, tripartite at the apex, with three long *stigmata.*

Fig. 1. Pistil, *magnified.*

5045.

W. Fitch del. et lith.

Vincent Brooks Imp.

Tab. 5045.

PENTSTEMON JAFFRAYANUS.

Mr. Jaffray's Pentstemon.

Nat. Ord. Scrophularineæ.—Didynamia Angiospermia.

Gen. Char. (*Vide supra*, Tab. 4318.)

Pentstemon *Jaffrayanus;* perennis erectus glaber glaucus, foliis omnino integerrimis, radicalibus spathulatis in petiolum brevem attenuatis, intermediis oblongo-ellipticis, supremis sensim minoribus sessilibus bracteisque cordato-ovatis, floribus pseudo-verticillatim paniculatis majusculis, calycis lobis late ovatis acutis, corollæ pulcherrime cærulææ basi fauceque rubræ limbo bilabiato, filamento sterili elongato imberbi.

My first knowledge of this lovely and hardy species of *Pentstemon* was derived from Mr. Jaffray's collections made at Clear Creek, North California, in 1853 (n. 1116 of his specimens). Seeds were at the same time sent home by him; but I know not if they ever germinated. Messrs. Veitch and Sons, of Exeter, and King's Road, Chelsea, have been more fortunate with Californian seeds of the same species they received from Mr. William Lobb; and in August, 1857, I had the pleasure to receive living specimens here represented. The *P. speciosus*, Douglas and Lindley (Bot. Reg. p. 1270), from the Strahan River, North-west America, is perhaps its nearest affinity, from which it is abundantly distinct, and is certainly more beautiful,—for there is that mixture in the corolla which is so unusual, viz. of bright blue and red, of which however we have an example in the Buglosses and some other Boragineous plants. This plant will assuredly form an interesting addition to our hardy herbaceous, and especially "bedding-out" plants. It continues to produce a succession of flowers in the summer months.

Descr. *Root* perennial. *Stems* erect, branching only below, about a foot high, young ones tinged with red, glabrous, as is every part of the plant. *Leaves* all very glaucous, entire; *lower leaves* spathulate, especially the *root-leaves*, and tapering below into a short petiole; intermediate ones oblong-elliptical, rather obtuse, not the least attenuated at the base, quite sessile, thence upwards they gradually become smaller and proportionally broader, ovato-cordate or cordate and quite sessile, acute. *Bracts* and *bracteoles* resembling these leaves, only still smaller. *Panicle* terminal. *Peduncles* opposite, two- or three- or more flowered; *flowers* moderately large and spreading, and thus pseudo-verticillate. *Calyx* short, of five deep, broad, ovate, acute, somewhat imbricated *lobes*, the apices patent. *Corolla* an inch and a quarter long, rich blue, red at the base and at the faux. *Limb* bilabiate, upper of two, lower of three, rounded spreading lobes. *Stamens* four, perfect, didynamous; *anthers* deep red. *Sterile filaments* almost as long as the perfect ones, beardless. *Ovary* narrow ovate. *Style* as long as the stamens. *Stigma obtuse.*

Fig. 1. Stamens. 2. Pistil:—*magnified.*

5046.

W. Fitch del et lith.

Vincent Brooks Imp.

Tab. 5046.

KEFERSTEINIA GRAMINEA.

Grass-leaved Kefersteinia.

Nat. Ord. Orchideæ.—Gynandria Monandria.

Gen. Char. Kefersteinia, *Reichb. fil.* *Perigonii* subpatuli *sepala* ac *petala* (*tepala*, Reichb.) oblongo-lanceolata, acuta, submembranacea. *Sepala* retrorsum oblique inserta. *Labellum* cum *gynostemii* pede producto articulatum, flabellatum seu rhombeum, cucullatum, basi callosum; *callo* laminato, foveato. *Gynostemium* semiteres, apice clavatum, rectum, marginibus lateralibus alatum, angulatum. *Androclinium* perpendiculare, ellipticum, immarginatum, apice rotundatum, *rostelli* tridentati dente medio subulato majore. *Stigma* lineare, transversum. *Crista* longitudinalis a stigmatis labio inferiori ad medium gynostemium (certe *staminodium* ent.). *Pollinia* pyriformia, papyracea, excavatula, per paria incumbentia, valde inæqualia, in *caudicula* obtusa ligulata, superne angulata, *glandula* oblonga infra adnata subæquilonga. *Reichb. fil.*

Kefersteinia *graminea;* labello transverso rhombeo apice retuso dimidio anteriori denticulato seu lacero fimbriato, callo rhombeo seu triangulo antice bilobo seu paucidentato a basi discum versus. *Reich. fil.*

Kefersteinia graminea. *Reichb. fil. in* "*V. Mohl, u. v. Schlecht. Bot. Zeit. x.* 634." *Xen. Orchid. p.* 67. *t.* 25. ii. *f.* 2–11.

Zygopetalum gramineum. *Lindl. Bot. Reg.* 1844, *Misc. p.* 15.

This curious Orchid was not known in cultivation when Dr. Lindley named and described it as *Zygopetalum gramineum.* It is from Popayan, on the west side of the Andes, where it was discovered by Hartweg, and it has since been found in the Caraccas by Linden, Funcke, and Schlim. We derived our plant from the Imperial Gardens of St. Petersburg, and we learn that it exists in gardens under the name of "*Huntleya fimbriata.*" Three species of the genus are described by Reichenbach fil.

Descr. *Pseudobulbs* none. The *leaves* rise directly from the root, and are about a span long, erect or spreading in a fan-shaped manner, lanceolate, moderately acuminated, faintly striated, carinated below, and jointed on to the compressed and conduplicate, equitant, sheathing bases. *Peduncles* also radical, springing from below the leaves, three to five, in a clustered manner, slender, almost filiform, weak, two to three inches long, flexuose, single-flowered, bracteated at the base, with a solitary *bract* near the middle, and a pair of opposite *bracts* beneath the single flower. Before expansion the peduncle almost rests on the ground, rising up (but never erect) as the flower expands. This *flower* is of a dirty-yellow colour, more or less copiously spotted with deep rich brown, the sepals and petals the palest, the large lip of the deepest colour; the whole reminds one very much of the colouring, and indeed somewhat of the shape, of a large *Aranea diadema*. *Sepals* and *petals* spreading horizontally, oblong-lanceolate, uniform, except that the petals are rather narrower. *Lip* broad oval: it can scarcely be said to be three-lobed; it is gibbous at the base beneath, concave in the centre above, the upper half suddenly bends downwards, and is emarginate at the apex, the edge crisped and minutely denticulate: at the base above is a large, four-lobed, fleshy gland (spotted like the rest of the lip), and, in our specimen, shaped somewhat like a butterfly with the wings expanded. *Column* elongated, semi-terete, carinated in front, the sides and carina unidentate near the middle; the back is slightly downy. *Anther* in face of the column. *Pollen-masses* four, club-shaped, attached to a triangular gland.

Fig. 1. Labellum. 2. Column and anther. 3. Pollen-masses:—*magnified*.

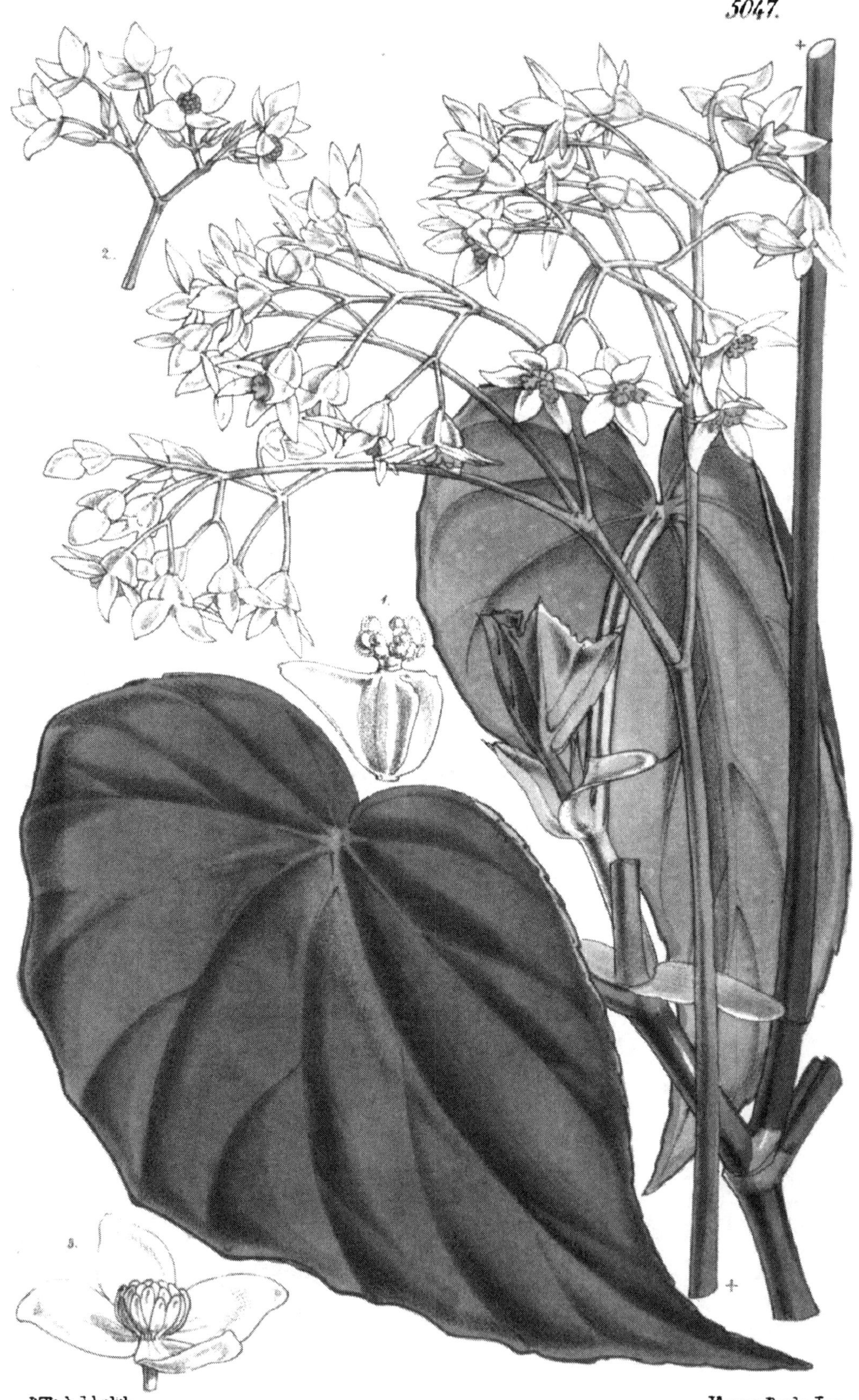

W. Fitch del et lith

Vincent Brooks Imp

Tab. 5047.

BEGONIA Wageneriana.

Mr. Wagener's Begonia.

Nat. Ord. Begoniaceæ.—Monœcia Polyandria.

Gen. Char. (*Vide supra*, Tab. 4172.)

Begonia *Wageneriana;* caule tereti erecto ramoso glaberrimo, foliis valde oblique ovatis acuminatis sinuatis hinc serratis, petiolo foliis subdimidio breviore, stipulis magnis oblongis obtusis apice longe mucronatis, pedunculis axillaribus longissimis, panicula multiflora dichotome cymosa, floribus parvis albis, masculis tetrasepalis, fœmineis pentasepalis, capsulæ alis duabus brevibus obtusis, tertia elongato-triangulari.

Moschkowitzia Wageneriana. *Klotzsch, Begon. p.* 76.

This may possess less beauty than many of the extensive genus *Begonia*, yet the deep yellow-green of the foliage, the rich colouring of the petioles and peduncles, and the very numerous, white, starry flowers, yellow in the centre, renders it a desirable inmate of the stove, and it continues blossoming for a long time in the early spring and summer. It is a native of Venezuela, and was introduced by Mr. Wagener to the Royal Botanic Gardens, Berlin, whence our plants have been derived.

Descr. *Plant* wholly glabrous. *Stem* erect, two and a half to three feet high, terete, somewhat zigzag, pale greenish-brown. *Leaves* five to six inches and more long, cordato-ovate, subfalcate, very unequally sided, subpeltate, acuminate, yellowish-green, paler beneath, one (the largest) side subangulato-sinuate at the margin, the other side and the acuminated apex serrated, veins prominent beneath. *Petioles* red, terete, erect, about half the length of the leaf. *Stipules* caducous, nearly an inch long, membranous, oblong, with a rather long mucro at the point. *Peduncles* axillary, very long, red, terete, succulent, bearing a much di-trichotomously branched cymose *panicle* of numerous small white *flowers*, sterile and fertile on different cymes. *Sterile flowers* of four, spreading, rather obtuse, white *sepals*. *Stamens* numerous, very compact, linear, yellow, collected into a nearly sessile globose head or ball. *Fertile flowers* of five, white, ovate, acute *sepals*, rather smaller than the sterile ones. *Capsule* obconical, with three unequal wings; two short, obtuse, and slightly denticulate; the third thrice as long, triangular, obtuse.

Fig. 1. Capsule, not quite mature, *magnified.* 2. Portion of a cyme, with sterile flowers, *nat. size.* 3. Sterile flower, *magnified.*

5048

Fitch del et lith.

Vincent Brooks Imp

Tab. 5048.

CATTLEYA granulosa.

Rough-lipped Cattleya.

Nat. Ord. Orchideæ.—Gynandria Monandria.

Gen. Char. (*Vide supra*, Tab. 2700.)

Cattleya *granulosa;* caulibus teretibus diphyllis, foliis oblongo-lanceolatis obtusis, petalis obovato-spathulatis undulatis obtusissimis, labello cucullato tripartito, laciniis lateralibus semiovatis intermedia sinu lato divulsa, ungue æquilatero lævi lamina rotundata plicata granulosa denticulata. *Lindl.*

Cattleya granulosa. *Lindl. Bot. Reg.* 1842, *v.* 28. *t.* 1.

β. Russelliana; foliis ovatis, pedunculis trifloris, floribus multo majoribus, petalis magis lanceolatis, labello ungue angustiore. *Lindl. Bot. Reg.* 1845, *v.* 31. *t.* 50.

Even a quarto plate scarcely suffices to do justice to a well-grown specimen of this noble *Cattleya.* Hartweg was the first to bring the species into notice, having sent it from Guatemala about 1840. It was figured by Dr. Lindley, with a solitary flower, from the only plant then known in Europe, in January, 1840. A three-flowered specimen then appeared in the same publication for 1845, as a variety, with somewhat broader leaves, as var. *Russelliana.* Our present specimen, with its noble cluster of flowers, was sent to us from the Botanic Garden, Liverpool, in 1845, by the late Mr. Henry Shepherd. Well cultivated as this specimen is, there are certainly few Orchideous plants that can surpass it in beauty. This flowered and was in perfection in August. Plants have also been sent from Guatemala by G. M. Skinner, Esq., who has contributed so largely to our collections in this family.

Descr. *Stems* or *pseudobulbs* a foot and more long, jointed at distant intervals, compressed and furrowed, and partially clothed with membranaceous *sheaths.* *Leaves* two, alternate (that is, there is a short portion of the stem, or pseudobulb, between them), oblong, patenti-reflexed, coriaceous, rather broad in the middle, sheathing only at the very base, obtuse at the point, dark green. *Peduncle* terminal, stout, terete, bearing a *spike* or *raceme* of six to eight large *flowers* at the extremity. *Sepals* and *petals* spreading, all of the same uniform olive yellowish-green colour, with a few, scattered, small, sanguineous spots; the *sepals* oblong, obtuse, even; the *petals* obovato-oblong, much waved at the margin. *Lip* white, fleshy, not so long as the sepals and petals, primarily three-lobed, the lateral lobes at the base rise like two auricles, and almost over the top of the column, they are yellow within; the middle lobe has a deep-orange spot at the base, is broad and oblong for a great part of the length, and spreading into a broad, somewhat reniform, waved, two-lobed extremity, and is covered with innumerable, deep rose-coloured *granulations,* from which circumstance the plant derives its specific name.

Fig. 1. Lip, *slightly magnified.*

5049.

W. Fitch del et lith

Vincent Brooks Imp.

Tab. 5049.

POLYGONATUM roseum.

Rose-flowered Solomon's-seal.

Nat. Ord. Smilacineæ.—Hexandria Monogynia.

Gen. Char. Perigonium corollaceum, tubulosum, limbo breviter sexfidum et erectiusculum, deciduum. *Stamina* 6, medio tubo inserta, inclusa. *Filamenta* tereti-subulata. *Antheræ* biloculares, lineari-oblongæ, emarginatæ, basi bifidæ, dorso medio affixæ, introrsæ. *Ovarium* liberum, sessile, triloculare; *ovula* in loculis 3–6, biseriata, anatropa. *Columna stylina* terminalis, erecta, elongata, trigona, inclusa. *Stigma* terminale, obsolete trilobum, supra papillosum. *Bacca* globosa, trilocularis. *Semina* in loculis 1–2, subglobosa. *Testa* tenuissima, albumini cartilagineo-carnoso arctissime adnata. *Embryo* parvus, tereti-oblongus, rectus, axilis, in extremitate albuminis chalaza opposita inclusus.—Rhizoma *horizontale, incrassatum.* Caulis *erectus, simplex, superne foliosus, inferne squamis vaginatus.* Folia *sessilia, sparsa, rarius opposita vel verticillata, striato-nervosa, nervis subtiliter reticulato-anastomosantibus, plerumque membranacea.* Pedunculi *axillares, solitarii, uni- vel racemoso-bi-pauciflori.* Flores *pedicellati, nutantes, albi, apice virides;* pedicellis *basi ebracteolatis vel bracteola minuta subulata instructis, sub flore articulatis. Kunth.*

Polygonatum *roseum;* caule teretiusculo subsulcato, foliis oblongo-linearibus v. lineari-lanceolatis acutiusculis apicibus rectis glabris, inferioribus subternis superioribus sparsis margine subtusque in nervis subtilissime scabriusculis, pedunculis axillaribus plerumque bifloris cernuis purpureo-roseis.

Polygonatum roseum. *Kunth, Enum. Pl. v.* 5. *p.* 141. *Ledeb. Fl. Ross. v.* 4. *p.* 123. *Schultz, Syst. Veget. v.* 7. *p.* 1669.

Convallaria rosea. *Ledeb. Fl. Altaic. v.* 2. *p.* 41; *Ic. Plant. Ross. t.* 1.

This very pretty *Polygonatum,* nearly allied to our *Polygonatum verticillatum,* was sent to the Royal Gardens by Professor Bunge, the friend of Professor Ledebour at Dorpat, and there is every reason to believe it is good authority for the plant so called of Ledebour in his 'Flora Rossica.' We have also authentic specimens in the herbarium from Professor Bunge. It is a native of the Altaic Siberia, at the river Kurtsch, and of Chinese Songaria, at Lake Saisang-Nor (Herb. Acad. Petrop. in Herb. Nostr.). But it must be confessed that the species varies considerably in the length and breadth of the leaves, and their being more or less verticillate, and if Ledebour's figure be correct, above quoted, in the size and colour of the flower. The species with which I would immediately compare it is the *Polygonatum Sibiricum* of Redouté's 'Liliacées,' figured there however from a dried and much shrivelled specimen. From this the *Convallaria cirrhifolia* of Wallich is not distinct. It is described as having the leaves almost uniformly verticillate, and with more or less cirrhose points. It is indeed extremely common in Himalaya, at elevations of from 7–11,000 feet (Hooker and Thomson); but specimens collected by Messrs. Strachey and Winterbottom, at Rinkim in Thibet, in our herbarium, gathered at an elevation of 13,500 feet above the sea, partake of the characters of the two species; the lower leaves being quite straight at the points, as in *P. roseum*, the upper ones with uncinate or slightly cirrhose points, a character so common in *P. Sibiricum;* so that unless the living plant were to exhibit some mark of distinction, it would be difficult to say to which of the two species this should be referred. The colour of the flowers seems to be the same in both. As neither one nor the other however has, as far as we know, been cultivated in our gardens, we gladly represent the *rosea* of Ledebour in our present Plate.

Descr. *Root* a horizontal, fleshy *tuber*, sometimes running out to a great length, and forming a long, fleshy *rhizome*, throwing up annual, simple, herbaceous, erect *stems*, one to two feet high, terete; but at the same time angular on the surface, pale whitish-green, sometimes tinged with red streaks. *Leaves* generally subverticillate but rarely strictly so, and here and there quite alternate, especially at the summit and at the very base, where indeed they almost constitute scales; in form the leaves are linear or linear-lanceolate, the uppermost ones slightly acuminated, striated, entire, the margins and keel under a high magnifier scaberulous. *Peduncles* axillary, solitary or two together, generally forked and two-flowered, sometimes bearing four flowers, rarely one. *Peduncle* and *pedicels* prettily mottled with dark-purple. *Perianth* in our living specimens about three-quarters of an inch long; the ground-colour is white, but slightly tinged with purple, mottled and streaked with pink, so that the general tint is rose-colour; the *tube* long; the *limb* of six, ovate, spreading segments, white at the margin and somewhat serrated or crested at the very apex. *Stamens* and *pistil* included. *Anthers* oblong, yellow. *Ovary* obovate. *Style* shorter than the ovary. *Stigma* truncated.

Fig. 1. Flower. 2. Pistil:—*magnified.*

W Fitch del et lith. Vincent Brooks Imp

Tab. 5050.

BOLBOPHYLLUM Neilgherrense.

Neilgherry Bolbophyllum.

Nat. Ord. Orchideæ.—Gynandria Monandria.

Gen. Char. (*Vide supra*, Tab. 4088.)

Bolbophyllum *Neilgherrense;* rhizomate repente, pseudobulbis ovatis angulatis subcorrugatis, folio solitario oblongo-elliptico obtusiusculo, scapo folio multo breviore, spica subcylindracea erecta, floribus laxiusculis erectis, bracteis lanceolatis herbaceis, sepalis lateralibus ovato-lanceolatis dorsali quadruplo majoribus, petalis parvis e basi ovata acuminatis purpurascentibus, labello recurvato trilobo, lobis lateralibus parvis intermedio lingulato integro, disco sulcato, columna utrinque alata, alis apice cuspidato-acuminatis.

Bolbophyllum Neilgherrense. *Wight, Ic. Plant. Ind. Or. v.* 5. *t.* 1650.

Our pseudobulbs of this plant were received from Mr. M'Ivor, who collected them in the Neilgherries in 1849; and Dr. Wight, the only author, as far as we know, who has noticed it, has given it as a native also of Malabar. That author alludes to its affinity with *Bolbophyllum Careyanum*, but considers it quite distinct, as may be seen by our figure of that species at our Tab. 4166. It flowered with us in January, 1858, in the warm Orchideous House.

Descr. *Pseudobulbs* oblongo-ovate, slightly compressed, partially clothed with a sheathing membrane, and arising from a creeping, jointed, sheathed *rhizome*, scarcely so thick as a goose-quill. *Leaf* solitary from the apex of the pseudobulb, four to six inches long, nearly erect, coriaceous, elliptical-oblong, rather obtuse, tapering below into a thickened, short *petiole*. *Scape* from the base of the pseudobulb, three to four inches long, terete, jointed, joints sheathed with a membrane. *Spike* scarcely three inches long, of several, erect, brownish-green, lax *flowers;* each flower subtended by a small, lanceolate, greenish *bract*. *Sepals* ovato-lanceolate; dorsal one small; lateral ones connivent at the base, so as to resemble the carina of a pa-

May 1st, 1858.

pilionaceous flower, four or five times as large as the dorsal one: *colour* brownish-green, spotted. *Petals* smaller even than the dorsal sepal, purplish, from a broad base, acuminate. *Lip* springing from the decurrent base of the column, and jointed upon it, recurved, three-lobed; lateral lobes small; intermediate one tongue-shaped, entire, furrowed down the middle. *Column* short, winged on each side, which wings terminate above in an acuminated point on each side the anther-case.

Fig. 1. Entire flower. 2. Flower from which the sepals and petals are removed, showing the column and the lip. 3. Pollen-masses:—*magnified.*

5051

W Fitch del et lith.

Vincent Brooks Imp

Tab. 5051.

CLIANTHUS Dampieri.

Dampier's Clianthus.

Nat. Ord. Leguminosæ.—Diadelphia Decandria.

Gen. Char. Calyx late campanulatus, subæqualis, 5-dentatus. *Vexillum* acuminatum, reflexum, alis parallelis longius; *carina* scapiformis, vexillo alisque multo longior, omnino monopetala. *Stamina* manifeste perigyna, diadelpha, omnia fertilia. *Stylus* staminibus duplo longior, versus apicem hinc leviter barbatus, stigmate simplicissimo. *Legumen* pedicellatum, coriaceum, acuminatum, ventricosum, polyspermum, intus lanulosum, sutura dorsali recta, ventrali convexa. *Semina* reniformia, funiculis longiusculis affixa.—Suffrutices herbææ; foliis *impari-pinnatis, stipulatis;* floribus *speciosissimis, racemosis. Lindl.*

Clianthus *Dampieri;* herbaceus prostratus sericeo-villosissimus, foliolis oppositis (rarissime alternis) oblongis passim lineari-oblongis obovatisve, pedunculis erectis scapiformibus, floribus subumbellatis, calycibus 5-fidis sinubus acutis, ovariis (leguminibusque immaturis) sericeis. *Br.*

Clianthus Dampieri. *All. Cunn. in Hort. Soc. Trans. ser.* 2. *v.* 1. *p.* 521. *Br. in App. to Sturt's Exped. to Central Australia, p.* 71.

Clianthus Oxleyi. *A. Cunn. in Hort. Soc. Trans. l. c. p.* 522.

Donia speciosa. *Don, Gard. Dict. v.* 2. *p.* 468.

Colutea Novæ-Hollandiæ. "*Woodw. in Dampier's Voy. v.* 3. *p.* 111. *t.* 4. *f.* 2."

From the Greenhouse of Messrs. Veitch and Sons, Exeter, and King's Road, Chelsea, where its splendid blossoms were produced in the month of March of the present year 1858. In point of size the flowers are quite equal to those of the now well-known *Clianthus puniceus*, but in richness of colour far superior, for the uniform crimson of the petals is relieved by the velvety purple-black disc of the standard of the petals. *Clianthus puniceus* is considered to be a native of New Zealand, though a decidedly wild locality has perhaps never yet been recorded.* This species

* Sir Joseph Banks and Dr. Solander, who were the first to notice this plant, in 1769, are said to have found it "on some part of the eastern coast of the Northern Island of New Zealand, or in Cook's Strait." Mr. Allan Cunningham observes, that this plant does not occur in a collection formed by his brother in New Zealand, and was not seen by himself during his first visit to

now under consideration is a native of New Holland, and was discovered so long ago as 1699, by Dampier (and published and figured by Woodward, in Dampier's Voyage, above quoted), in the dry sandy islands of Dampier's Archipelago, North-west Australia, latitude 29° 19′ to 20° 30′, longitude 116° to 117° east. Allan Cunningham gathered it in the same locality in 1818. Specimens from near that group of islands, namely on the "north-west coast of Australia," are in my herbarium, gathered by Mr. Bynoe in the voyage of H.M.S. Beagle. Again, Mr. Allan Cunningham met with the same plant in the western interior of New South Wales, on the eastern shore of Regent's Lake on the river Lachlan. The same plant was observed on the Gawler Range, not far from the head of Spencer's Gulf, in 1839, by Mr. Eyre, and more recently by Captain Sturt, on his "Barriere Range, near the Darling, about 500 feet above the river." Mr. Brown has examined specimens from all these localities, and is satisfied that they belong to one and the same species.

Mr. Brown, judging from the unripe pods in my herbarium, was of opinion that this would, when the perfect pods were known to us, prove to be sufficiently distinct from the original New Zealand species to form a distinct genus, but the pods and the seeds seem to exhibit no difference as far as can be judged from the immature state, save in the absence of the woolly substance in the former. The seeds are rather numerous, and are each on a long podosperm.

On the first exhibition of this charming plant at the Horticultural Society, a silver medal was most justly awarded to Messrs. Veitch and Son.

DESCR. A procumbent or ascending, herbaceous *plant*, glaucous, and hoary all over with long, whitish, silky hair. *Stems* slightly angular and tinged with red. *Leaves* alternate, pinnated, petiolated, oblong, with about sixteen rather closely placed subopposite, oblong or elliptical, frequently acute, sessile leaflets; *petiole* one to three inches long, with a pair of large, herbaceous, bifid stipules at the base. *Peduncle* terminal, sometimes a span long, bearing a racemose *umbel* of four to six, very large, drooping flowers. *Pedicels* bibracteolate. *Calyx* hairy, with the tube

the Northern Island in 1826. It is probably a rare plant, and its peculiar localities are to the southward of the Bay of Islands, where Allan Cunningham subsequently gathered it; it also occurs on the shores of the River Thames, at Mercury Bay, where Cook afforded the naturalists who accompanied that voyage the opportunity of landing, in 1769, and near which, namely at Tauranga, in the Bay of Plenty, are the Missionaries' Home Stations, whence the first seeds were sent to Europe, and raised by W. Leveson Gower, Esq., of Titsey Place, Godstone. Dr. Hooker, in his 'Flora Novæ Zelandiæ,' gives the locality of Banks and Solander, and says, "more generally cultivated."

cup-shaped, obtuse at the base; *segments* five, nearly equal, erecto-patent, lanceolate, acuminate. *Corolla* bright-red. *Standard* very large, ovato-lanceolate, suddenly from above the base curved upwards, so that it presents its inner surface to the spectator in front, and this exhibits a double or two-lobed projection at the base of the disc, very prominent, and of a purplish velvety black colour, gradually melting into the red, and reflecting a strong light from the apex of its lobes. *Wings* small, lanceolato-subulate, deflexed; *keel* very large, deflexed, lanceolato-falcate, acuminate, longer than the standard. *Stamens* diadelphous, nine united and one free, very long. *Anthers* linear. *Ovary* pedicellate, hairy, linear, gradually tapering into the long, subulate *style*.

Fig. 1. Stamens and pistil. 2. Pistil removed from the receptacle:—*magnified*.

W. Fitch del et lith. Vincent Brooks Imp.

TAB. 5052.

FRITILLARIA GRÆCA.

Greek Fritillary.

Nat. Ord. LILIACEÆ.—HEXANDRIA MONOGYNIA.

Gen. Char. (*Vide supra*, TAB. 3280.)

FRITILLARIA *Græca;* glabra *glauca*, caule humili basi nudo dein 5–8-phyllo, foliis omnibus alternis, inferioribus approximatis *oblongis vel oblongo-lanceolatis* obtusis acutiusculisve, summis remotioribus anguste linearibus acutis, floribus mediocribus 1 rarius 2 terminalibus nutantibus ultimo foliosis breviori approximatis, perigonii breviter campanulati basi rotundati non gibbosi diametro suo æquilongi phyllis extus fascia viridi-lutescente longitudinali percursis, cæterum rubris obscure tessellatis ellipticis apice rotundato vel subattenuato obtuso vel subretuso pilosulis, nectario oblongo-lineari, staminibus corolla dimidio brevioribus, *filamentis glabris* e basi dilatata attenuatis anthera breviter apiculata duplo longioribus, stylo glabro longitudinis ovarii stamina paululum superante ad medium usque trifido. *Boiss.*

FRITILLARIA Græca. *Boiss. et Sprunner in Boiss. Diagnos. Plant. Orient. Nov. n.* 7. 1846, *p.* 104.

FRITILLARIA tulipifolia. *Fl. Græca, non M. Bieb.* (*Boiss. in Herb. Nostr.*)

A native of Mount Hymettus, about the middle of the mountain, and hardy in our gardens. Of this pretty Fritillary, like the Rose-flowered Solomon's-seal of this number, Tab. 5049, we have the advantage of possessing authentic living plants, derived from M. Boissier's garden at Geneva, and from which our figures have been taken. They flower readily in the open border, and in a frame in the month of March, when flowers are always welcome. Long as is the specific character given by Boissier and Sprunner, it is only justice to the authors of the species to give their own words: for indeed so closely is it allied to *F. tulipifolia* of Bieberstein, Centur. Plant. Ross. tab. 41, that I should have a difficulty in distinguishing the two except by the markings of the flowers;—in *F. tulipifolia* all tessellated, very much like *F. Meleagris*; in *F. Græca* scarcely tessellated, and having a green line down the centre of each sepal. In one of our native specimens, however, also "e monte Hymetto Atticæ," from Heldreich, marked as a *var.*, the green line is quite obsolete, and the whole perianth is a chocolate-brown. The most essential distinguishing characters, we presume, are given above in italics. It is only in a note upon specimens from Boissier himself, in our herbarium, that he has attached the remark that this plant is the *F. tulipifolia* of 'Flora Græca,' not of M. Bieberstein: that synonym is not given in the 'Diagnoses.'

DESCR. *Root* a small, subglobose *bulb*. *Stem* a span (more or less) high, slender, erect, terete. *Root-leaves* from young bulbs four to five inches long, lanceolate, tapering into a *petiole*. Cauline *leaves*, in our plants and specimens, four to six or seven in number, mostly five, elliptical or linear-lanceolate, nearly erect, striated, the upper ones gradually smaller, uppermost one arising from the base of the peduncle. *Flowers* solitary, rarely two, smaller than those of *F. Meleagris*, and less campanulate. *Sepals* elliptical, slightly apart when fully open, tawny or ferruginous-brown, spotted but scarcely tessellated, with a dorsal green line continued to the projection which constitutes the nectary at the base; the margin is also pale-green. *Stamens* shorter than the sepals, and rather shorter than the pistil. *Ovary* oblong. *Style* short, longer than the ovary, and nearly twice as long as the branches of the style.

Fig. 1. Sepals, with nectary. 2. Pistil:—*magnified*.

W Fitch del et lith.

Vincent Brooks Imp.

Tab. 5053.

DENDROBIUM chrysotoxum.

Golden-arched Dendrobium.

Nat. Ord. Orchideæ.—Gynandria Monandria.

Gen. Char. (*Vide supra*, Tab. 4755.)

Dendrobium (§ Dendrocoryne) *chrysotoxum*; pseudobulbis angustis multicostatis 2–4-foliis, foliis oblongis horizontalibus coriaceis, racemis lateralibus laxis gracilibus arcuatim decurvis pseudobulbos æquantibus, bractea basilari parva spathacea floralibus minimis herbaceis, sepalis petalisque explanatis oblongis obtusissimis planis bis duplo latioribus, labello indiviso cucullato rotundato pubescente margine minutissime pectinato et fimbriato. *Lindl.*

Dendrobium (§ Dendrocoryne) chrysotoxum. *Lindl. in Bot. Reg.* 1847, *sub t.* 19.

The *Dendrocoryne* section of the fine East Indian genus *Dendrobium* forms, Dr. Lindley observes, "a peculiar group, best perhaps characterized by their having a fleshy, angular stem, with two or more manifest articulations, one or more leaves at the upper end, and a lip not broken up into a tuft of hairs or fringes. They are, as it were, *Bolbophylla* passing into *Dendrobia*. In the group thus limited are included *D. densiflorum*, *Griffithii*, *aggregatum*, *tetragonum*, *Veitchianum*, *speciosum*, and some others formerly placed in *Desmotrichum*, a species whose lip is broken up into a brush."

Our plant here figured is certainly not among the least handsome in this lovely group, and was imported from India by Messrs. Henderson. It flowers with us in March, and is highly ornamental to the stove at that season.

Descr. *Pseudobulbs* long, clustered, clavate or rather spindle-shaped, jointed, with elongated joints, and clothed with a compact, whitish, membranaceous sheath, having about four, more or less spreading, oblong, acute, coriaceous, dark-green *leaves* at the extremity. *Peduncle* lateral, arising from the top of the pseudobulb, just below the leaves, rather short, bearing a gracefully drooping *raceme* of twelve or more, large, golden-yellow *flowers*; almost a span long. There is a deciduous, scariose, sheathing *bract* at the base of the peduncle, and a very small one at the base of each ovary. The *flowers* are two inches across. *Sepals* and *petals* spreading; the former rather small, oval or oblong-oval; the latter broad-ovate, twice as large as the sepals, slightly twisted. *Lip* spreading, undivided, cucullate, the base contracted, having a prominent blunt *spur* behind, the lamina orbicular, pubescent on the upper surface, the margin most beautifully fringed and ciliated: the colour of the lip is of the same deep bright-yellow as the rest of the flower, but the disc above is orange-colour, leaving a pale margin, and an arch or semicircle of very deep orange is seen at the base of the lamina, which suggested the specific name of the plant. *Column* short, with a broad blunt tooth on each side the anther-case.

Fig. 1. Column and anther. 2. Portion of the fringe of the lip:—*magnified*.

5054

5054.

W. Fitch del et lith.

Vincent Brooks Imp.

TAB. 5054.

RHODODENDRON ARGENTEUM.

Silver-leaved Rhododendron.

Nat. Ord. ERICEÆ.—DECANDRIA MONOGYNIA.

Gen. Char. (*Vide supra*, TAB. 4336.)

RHODODENDRON *argenteum;* foliis amplis coriaceis oblongo-obovatis acutis in petiolum crassum attenuatis planis utrinque glaberrimis subtus argenteis, costa nervisque prominulis, bracteis deciduis dense sericeis, floribus capitatis, pedunculis brevibus crassis puberulis, calyce brevissimo obscure lobato, corollæ demum albæ majusculæ tubo campanulato, limbi lobis 8 breviusculis bilobis, staminibus 10–15, filamentis basin versus glanduloso-pubescentibus, ovarii pubescentis loculis 10–16, stylo flexuoso crasso, stigmate dilatato.

RHODODENDRON argenteum. *Hook. fil. Rhod. Sik. Himal. p.* 10. *t.* 9.

A tree, in its native country, thirty feet in height, a native of Sikkim-Himalaya; on the summit of Sinchul, Suradah, and Tonglo, elev. 8,000–10,000 feet above the level of the sea; and certainly among the finest of the many fine Rhododendron-discoveries of Dr. Hooker. Even in its flowerless state it is a noble plant on account of its foliage, the leaves being often a foot in length, and broad in proportion, always silvery beneath. Another interesting state is in the early spring, when the new leaf-buds are forming; these are long, and clothed with coloured, imbricated, large scales, so as to look, as Dr. Hooker remarks, like the cone of some species of Pine; the outer or lower scales broad and coriaceous, glabrous, reddish-brown; the innermost ones oblongo-spathulate, pubescent. Still more interesting is the plant with its head of handsome flowers, pink in bud, gradually whitening as they expand, and having at the base of the tube within, a rich, dark, blood-purple spot surrounding the stamens, quite conspicuous on a full front view of the flower. The flowers were, as far as we know, now produced for the first time in cultivation, in a cool greenhouse of the Royal Gardens, in March, 1858.

JUNE 1ST, 1858.

Descr. Our *plants* are from four to five feet high, erect. *Leaves* very much confined to the summits of the branches, oblongo-obovate, coriaceous, conspicuous, penninerved; the nerves sunk, dark full green above, beneath silvery-white. *Flower-buds* imbricated with large, brown, very broad, obtuse *scales*. *Flowers* capitate, compact. *Peduncles* very short, subumbellate, thick, curved downwards. *Calyx* literally none, unless about six small *bracteoles*, reflexed bodies bent down upon the peduncle, can be so called; these have their origin at the very top of the peduncle (under the very base of the corolla), and are linear or oblong, white, somewhat fleshy, occasionally divided into two unequal segments. *Corolla* in bud fine rose-colour, obovate compressed, deeply eight-furrowed; as the corolla expands it gradually changes to white, and is then broad, tubular-campanulate, two and a quarter inches long, laterally a little compressed; *tube* slightly widening upwards, eight-furrowed, discoloured at the base in consequence of a large, black-purple, velvety, eight-rayed spot, at the bottom within, surrounding the stamens. *Limb* spreading, two and a quarter inches in diameter, eight-lobed; *lobes* rounded, imbricated, deeply emarginate, almost bifid, slightly lobed or waved. *Stamens* sixteen. *Filaments* compacted almost into a tube below, white, slender, as long as the tube of the corolla, slightly curved upwards from the base, and there hairy. *Anther* small, oblong, rich red-brown, opening by two pores at the apex. *Pollen* white. *Ovary* ovate-oblong, ten-furrowed, woolly. *Style* as long as the stamens, set abruptly on to the top of the ovary; the apex clubbed, and curving upwards. *Stigma* a large, fleshy-coloured, oval disc, with a depressed line in the centre.

Fig. 1. Flower, *nat. size*, with the five bracteoles (?) at the base of the corolla. 2. Stamen. 3. Pistil. 4. Transverse section of the ovary, seated upon the fleshy disc.

5055.

TAB. 5055.

XIPHIDIUM FLORIBUNDUM.

Copious-flowered Xiphidium.

Nat. Ord. WACHENDORFIACEÆ.—TRIANDRIA MONOGYNIA.

Gen. Char. Perianthium corollinum, hexaphyllum; *foliolis* patentibus, exterioribus dorso puberulis, interioribus paulo minoribus glabris. *Stamina* 3, hypogyna, *perigonii foliolis* interioribus opposita; *filamenta* filiformia; *antheræ* basifixæ. *Ovarium* liberum, trigonum, triloculare. *Ovula* in placentis e loculorum angulo centrali tumentibus, plurima, amphitropa. *Stylus* filiformis; *stigma* capitato-trilobum. *Capsula* subglobosa, carnoso-mollis, trilocularis. *Semina* plurima, subglobosa.—Herba *perennis in America tropica cis Æquatorem obvia;* radice *fibrosa;* caule *simplici, hirsutiusculo, basi folioso;* foliis *ensiformibus, equitantibus, acuminatis, integerrimis v. subserrulatis;* floribus *paniculatis, subsecundis, nutantibus. Endl.*

XIPHIDIUM *floribundum.*

XIPHIDIUM floribundum. *Sw. Prodr. p.* 17; *Fl. Ind. Occ. v.* 1. *p.* 80. *t.* 2. *Vahl, Enum. v.* 2. *p.* 162. *Ræm. et Schult. Syst. Veget. v.* 1. *p.* 487.

a. albiflorum; floribus albidis. *Sw.* (TAB. NOSTR. 5055.)

XIPHIDIUM albidum. *Lam. Ill. v.* 1. *p.* 131. *Spreng. Syst. Veget. v.* 1. *p.* 170.

XIPHIDIUM album. *Willd. Sp. Pl. v.* 1. *p.* 249.

IXIA Xiphidium. *Læfl. It. p.* 179.

β. cæruleum; floribus intus cæruleis. *Sw.*

XIPHIDIUM cæruleum. *Aubl. Guian. v.* 1. *p.* 33. *t.* 11. *Willd. Sp. Pl. v.* 1. *p.* 24.

XIPHIDIUM giganteum. *Lindl. Bot. Reg. v.* 32, *under t.* 60, *and v.* 33, *under t.* 1.

This is a little-known plant, peculiar to tropical America, remarkable for its equitant leaves and Iris-like habit, with only three stamens, but having a regular floral envelope of six pieces, and a superior ovary, as in *Asphodeleæ*. Its affinity is naturally with *Wachendorfia*, and these two genera have generally been placed in *Hæmodoraceæ;* but Mr. Herbert has established for them the Nat. Ord. *Wachendorfiaceæ*, which is preserved by Lindley, though the position of this Order is not very clearly determined. The species, too, have apparently been needlessly multiplied; and it is generally acknowledged that the blue- and white-flowering kinds are mere varieties of each other; while Dr. Lindley's *Xiphidium*, being identical with our plant, derived from the same source, Santa Martha (Mr. Purdie), is simply a larger specimen than usual, with leaves obsoletely serrated. Besides the localities for this species given by Aublet and Swartz, namely French Guiana, Vera Cruz, islands of Tobago and St. Christopher, I may add, from my herbarium, Plain of Dapur, Santa Martha, Surinam, British Guiana, Antioquia, New Granada (Holton), Mecapulco, Mexico, and Dominica, St. Vincent, and Jamaica of the West Indian Islands.

Descr. *Rhizome* long, descending, jointed, thick as a swan's quill, radicant and sending out offsets. *Stems* apparently annual, herbaceous, from a few inches to a foot or more long, erect, compressed, unbranched, but not unfrequently proliferous from buds in the axils of the leaves, glabrous, leafy. *Leaves* alternate equitant, sword-shaped, the flattened base forming a short *sheath* upon the stem (as in *Iris*), from eight or ten inches to a foot and a half long, one to two inches and more broad, distichous, membranaceous, closely striated, more or less distinctly but finely spinuloso-serrate, especially towards the acuminated apex. *Peduncle* terminal, bracteated, bearing an oblong *thyrsus* or compound raceme of flowers, from four to six or eight inches long; *racemelets* spreading, subscorpioid; the *flowers* six to eight, all on the upper side, gradually opening from below, hairy or glabrous. *Pedicles* bracteolated, short. *Perianth* of six, white, spreading, oblong-oval *sepals*, regular. *Stamens* as long as the pistil, three, erect, from the base of the inner sepals. *Filaments* short, glabrous. *Anther* oblong, orange-colour. *Ovary* quite superior, globose, obscurely three-lobed. *Style* twice as long as the ovary. *Stigma* obtuse. Both in our cultivated specimens and in all our numerous native ones in the herbarium, the ovary falls off without coming to maturity, the plant apparently increasing mainly by lateral buds from the stem.

Fig. 1. Flower. 2. Pistil:—*magnified.*

5056.

W. Fitch del et lith

Vincent Brooks Imp.

Tab. 5056.

OBERONIA acaulis.

Stemless Oberonia.

Nat. Ord. Orchideæ.—Gynandria Monandria.

Gen. Char. (*Vide supra*, Tab. 4517.)

Oberonia *acaulis;* curvato-dependens, foliis ensiformibus e basi sensim longe acuminatis, racemo elongato multifloro, floribus compactis subverticillatis, sepalis petalisque subspiraliter patenti-reflexis, labello 4-lobo margine fimbriato facie superiore pilis sparsis villosis, lobis obtusis duobus terminalibus majoribus, disco canaliculato.

Oberonia acaulis. *Griff. in Notulæ ad Plantas Asiat. pars* 3. *p.* 275; *Itin. Notes, p.* 76; *Ic. Plant. Asiat. t.* 286. *v.* 1.

The genus *Oberonia* will prove a very extensive one in species, though comparatively few are as yet accurately described. Dr. Lindley has kindly referred us to the *Oberonia acaulis*, Griff., for the present species. It is rudely figured by Griffith, l.c., and the dissections are still more rude; but the identity of the two is confirmed by an original specimen in Dr. Lindley's herbarium. It is a native of Churra, in Khasya, Eastern Bengal, and is one of the many interesting Orchideous plants the introduction of which to our gardens we owe to Mr. Simons. It flowered with us in February of the present year.

Descr. The habit of this plant is very peculiar. Cultivated on a small block of wood, and suspended from the roof of the Orchideous house, it takes a downward curvature, so that the leaves and orange-coloured raceme are strongly curvato-pendent. *Leaves* stemless, few, the longest of them a foot long, ensiform, falcately recurved, gradually tapering from the base into a long acumen, scarcely an inch broad in the widest part; their bases equitant, in colour glaucous-green. *Peduncle* three to four inches long, rather stout, terminal. *Raceme* long, cylindrical, almost equal in length to the leaves, with very numerous orange-coloured (but not bright) *flowers*, compact, but much less so and by no

June 1st, 1858.

means so small as in our *O. iridifolia* (Tab. 4517). *Bracteas* oblong-acute, serrated at the apex. *Sepals* and *petals* uniform, ovate, fimbriato-ciliate, singularly reflexed, so as to be on the same plane with the labellum, with an exactly opposite direction, and at the same time slightly spirally twisted. *Lip* subquadrangular, obtusely four-lobed, or, in other words, three-lobed; middle lobe much the largest and broadest, and itself two-lobed; all obtuse, and all fimbriato-ciliate; and the same soft hairs of the margin extend to the surface of the lip: the disc is channelled. *Column* very short. *Anther-case* hemispherical. *Pollen-masses* two.

Fig. 1. Bractea. 2, 3. Flowers. 4. Pollen-masses :—*magnified.*

W Fitch del et lith

Vincent Brooks Imp

TAB. 5057.

POLYGALA HILAIRIANA.

St. Hilaire's Milkwort.

Nat. Ord. POLYGALACEÆ.—DIADELPHIA OCTANDRIA.

Gen. Char. Calycis sepala persistentia, 2 interiora alæformia. *Petala* 3–5, tubo stamineo connexa, inferiore carinæformi (forsan e duobus coalitis constante). *Capsula* compressa, elliptica, obovata aut obcordata. *Semina* pubescentia, *hilo* carunculata, coma destituta. *De Cand.*

POLYGALA (§ Ecristata) *Hilairiana;* frutex, caule simplici superne folioso, foliis oblongo-ovatis acutiusculis coriaceis basi in petiolum attenuatis, spicis axillaribus terminalibusque folio brevioribus, floribus (inter maximos) sessilibus basi minute bibracteatis, calyce clauso, sepalis duobus interioribus corolla paulo brevioribus suboblique ovatis paululum falcatis, corolla imberbi, petalis 2 linearibus intermedio apice cucullato trilobo, ovario subrotundo emarginato.

POLYGALA Hilairiana. *Endl. in Linnæa, v. 7. p. 357. Atakt. Bot. v. 4. t. 4. Walp. Repert. Bot. Syst. v. 1. p. 242.*

Received at the Royal Gardens of Kew from Mr. Mackay, of Liége, under the name of *Polygala Brasiliensis*, a species, if we may judge from the brief and only character (of less than two lines in De Candolle's 'Prodromus'), with characters totally at variance from this now under consideration, which is, however, unquestionably identical with the *Polygala Hilairiana* of Endlicher, of which we possess specimens from South Brazil, gathered by Sellow. It is also in the Benthamian Herbarium, from Martius (n. 1186). It is perhaps the largest-flowered species of the genus. Some of our leaves are fully a span long, and the flowers are quite an inch long. Yet although the leaves are large and evergreen, the flowers present but little show or beauty. Endlicher gives it as an inhabitant of the neighbourhood of Bahia. It flowers in the stove during the spring months.

DESCR. *Stem* unbranched, erect, a foot high in our flowering plants, terete, woody below, herbaceous above, where alone the plant is leafy, glabrous, as is every part of the plant. *Leaves* in our growing specimens four to five inches, in our native specimens a span long, subcoriaceous, oblongo-ovate, subacute, penninerved, entire, tapering below into a short petiole, all alternate. *Racemes* spicate, solitary, axillary and terminal, shorter than the leaves, erect, six- to eight- or ten-flowered. *Flowers* the largest of the genus. *Pedicels* short. *Calyx* of five sepals, three outer very small, green, ovate, of which two are combined and unequally bifid. Two inner *sepals* corolloid, white, with a tinge of green and black, obliquely ovate, a little falcate, obscurely nerved, three-quarters of an inch long, both close-pressed to the corolla. *Corolla* a little longer than the inner sepals (or *alæ*); inner *petals* combined for the greater portion of their length into a tube, white and compressed. Lateral *petals* linear, subacute, intermediate one cucullate and three-lobed, and rose-coloured at the apex. *Stamens* also combined into a tube; the *filaments* free above. *Anther* ovate. *Ovary* orbicular, compressed, emarginate. *Style* filiform, curved upwards, and clavate towards the apex. *Stigma* cleft.

Fig. 1. Calyx and pistil, the corolla removed. 2. Corolla. 3. Stamens:—*magnified*.

5058.

W Fitch del et lith

Vincent Brooks Imp

TAB. 5058.

DENDROBIUM FALCONERI; var. *sepalis petalisque obtusioribus.*

Dr. Falconer's Dendrobium: with sepals and petals more obtuse.

Nat. Ord. ORCHIDEÆ.—GYNANDRIA MONANDRIA.

Gen. Char. (*Vide supra*, TAB. 4755.)

DENDROBIUM (§ Dendromyce) *Falconeri;* caulibus hic illic ramosis elongatis pendulis gracilibus striatis articulatis geniculis nodosis, foliis paucis parvis 1–3 terminalibus linearibus, pedicellis solitariis unifloris, floribus amplis speciosis, sepalis oblongo-lanceolatis subtortilibus petalisque ovatis æquilongis patentibus apice purpureo-maculatis, labello cucullato, limbo vix trilobo ovato acuto undulato integerrimo ciliato, disco aurantiaco basi apiceque purpureis, calcare brevissimo.

DENDROBIUM Falconeri. *Hook. Bot. Mag. t.* 4944.

β; foliis minoribus, petalis sepalisque obtusioribus, maculis purpurascentibus minoribus. (TAB. NOSTR. 5055.)

From the nursery of Messrs. Jackson, where it produced its beautiful and richly-marked flowers in March, 1858. It is one of the many East Indian or, more correctly speaking, Assam and Khasya *Orchideæ*, sent to Europe by Mr. Simons, and which are now the grace and ornament of our stoves. Elegant as is our present plant, it cannot be considered as a species distinct from the *D. Falconeri* above quoted, but the flowers are smaller, the apices of the sepals and petals less acuminated, and the purple spots are all smaller and almost obsolete on the apex of the lip.

DESCR. *Stems* or *pseudobulbs* aggregated, singularly long and slender, articulated, jointed, the articulations very unequal in length, often contracted in the middle, leafy only towards the extremity. *Leaves* scarcely longer than one's finger, subdistichous, oblongo-lanceolate, rather finely acuminated and unequally bifid at the apex, between membranaceous and coriaceous, rather long-sheathed at the base. *Flowers* very handsome, subfasciculated at the joints of the long, pendent, leafless stems.

Bracteas membranaceous, oblong. The ground-colour of the rather large *flowers* is white. *Sepals* oval, oblong, acute, spreading, tipped with purple. *Petals* also spreading and equally tipped with purple, broad-ovate. *Lip* cucullate, shortly spurred at the base behind, scarcely three-lobed, broad; the *disc* rich-yellow and pubescent, having a deep sanguineous spot near the base and a small purple spot at the apex; the margin at the base is fringed. *Ovary* slightly clavate, pedunculiform. *Column* short, decumbent at the base to where the lip is jointed upon it, bearing a tooth on each side at the top. *Anther-case* white, hemispherical.

Fig. 1. Column and anther-case, *magnified*.

5059.

W. Fitch del. et lith.

Vincent Brooks Imp.

Tab. 5059.

ILEX cornuta.

Horned-leaved Holly.

Nat. Ord. Ilicineæ.—Tetrandria Monogynia.

Gen. Char. Flores hermaphroditi v. rarius polygami. *Calyx* parvus, urceolatus, quadridentatus, rarius 5–6-dentatus, persistens. *Corolla* hypogyna, rotata, 4-partita, rarius 5–6-partita, laciniis obtusis æstivatione imbricatis. *Stamina* imæ corollæ inserta, ejusdem laciniis numero æqualia et alterna; *filamenta* filiformia; *antheræ* introrsæ, biloculares, longitudinaliter dehiscentes. *Ovarium* sessile, 4-loculare. *Ovula* in loculis solitaria v. interdum gemina, collateralia, ex apice anguli centralis pendula, anatropa. *Stigmata* 4, sessilia, distincta v. coalita. *Drupa* baccata, subglobosa, stigmatibus coronata, tetrapyrena, *pyrenis* osseis venosis monospermis. *Semina* inversa, subtriquetra, testa tenuissime membranacea. *Embryo* in apice albuminis carnosi, sulco longitudinali bipartiti, minimus, subglobosus, bilobus; *radicula* supera.—Arbusculæ *v.* frutices *in America tropica et boreali, in Asia calidiore, et in insulis Canariis obviæ, una species etiam in Europa media et boreali-occidentali indigena;* foliis *alternis, coriaceis, crenatis v. spinoso-dentatis;* pedunculis *axillaribus, uni-multifloris, bracteatis;* floribus *albis. Endl.*

Ilex *cornuta;* foliis oblongis coriaceis marginatis basi obtusis apice truncatis, in planta vegetiore grosse sinuato-dentatis spinosis in adultis tricornis integrisque, umbellis axillaribus sessilibus, baccis tetrapyrenis. *Lindl. et Paxt.*

Ilex cornuta. *Lindl. et Paxt. Fl. Gard. v.* 1. *p.* 43. *f.* 27 (*woodcut only*). *Gard. Chron.* 1851, *p.* 311. *Walp. Ann. Bot. Syst. v.* 2. *p.* 265.

This extremely handsome-leaved species of Holly was detected by Mr. Fortune, when he was in the service of the Horticultural Society, in northern China, somewhere in the vicinity of Shanghai, flowering in April; and, upon another visit, at a place called Kin-tang. It was apparently on the latter occasion that this fine evergreen was sent living to Messrs. Standish and Co., Bagshot Nursery, to whom the merit of its introduction is due. It promises to be quite hardy; but it is only our young plants kept under glass, in a cool frame, that have shown any disposition to flower, and these flowers are produced in April.

Descr. Our flowering specimens are quite young and small, a foot and a half high; but to what size the species ultimately attains in its native country we have no information. In its mode of ramification it resembles our common European Holly; but the foliage is extremely different, and very peculiar. The *leaves* are alternate, two to four inches long, very firm, coriaceous, and glossy, dark blackish-green above; the general outline is broad-oblong, almost a parallelogram, on short petioles, truncated at the base and at the apex, bearing a strong spine on each side near the base; the apex is dilated and furnished with three larger and broader and very pungent spines, of which the intermediate one takes a downward curvature, while the lateral ones stand out horizontally, like two horns, and these have suggested the specific name; the margin of the leaf between these several spines is recurved. *Flowers* white, quite destitute of beauty, collected into sessile *umbels* in the axils of the younger leaves. *Peduncles* short, glabrous. *Calyx* cup-shaped, half superior, the free portion cut into four, erecto-patent, rounded *lobes*. *Petals* four, oblong, obtuse, horizontally patent. *Stamens* four, erecto-patent. *Filaments* very long, stout, subulate. *Anthers* ovate, obtuse. The *ovary* has four nearly sessile stigmas. The *berries* are described as being large, globose, with four *pyrenæ*.

Fig. 1. Entire flower. 2. Calyx and pistil:—*magnified*.

5060.

Tab. 5060.

RHODODENDRON virgatum.

Twiggy Rhododendron.

Nat. Ord. Ericeæ.—Decandria Monogynia.

Gen. Char. (*Vide supra*, Tab. 4336.)

Rhododendron *virgatum*; erecta, ramis gracilibus, ramulis junioribus calyce ovario petiolis foliisque subtus squamulis peltatis obsitis, foliis oblongis acutis brevi-petiolatis subtus glaucescentibus, floribus axillis foliorum terminalium singulo bracteato, bracteis amplis imbricatis, lobis calycinis rotundatis ciliatis, corollæ tubo infundibuliformi dorso villoso, limbi patentis lobis late ovatis, staminibus 8–10, filamentis inferne villosis, ovario 5-loculari.

Rhododendron virgatum. *Hook. fil. Rhod. Sik. Himal. t.* 26 *A. Journ. Hort. Soc. Lond. v.* 7. *p.* 81 (*excluding the syn. of* R. triflorum, *Hook. fil.*).

One of the many interesting *Rhododendron* discoveries of Dr. Hooker in Sikkim-Himalaya, where it abounds in the skirts of the Pine-forests in ravines at elevations of 8000 to 9000 feet of the Lachen Valley. Mr. Booth detected the same plant in similar localities in Bhotan, and the flowering-specimen here figured is from the garden of Mr. Lowe, of the Clapton Nursery, having been raised from seeds sent by Mr. Booth to Mr. Nuttall. It flowered in April, in a cool frame. Dr. Hooker was probably in error in considering his *R. triflorum* to be a yellow-flowered variety of the present. The leaves and inflorescence are considerably different.

Descr. This may be reckoned among the dwarfish kinds of the genus, not rising more than a foot and a half high, but with graceful, slender, *twiggy* branches (whence the specific name), the new shoots being covered with copious, orbicular, peltate *scales*. Similar *scales* occur, and equally copiously, on the under side of the leaves, on the petioles, base of the calyx, and on the ovary. *Leaves* scattered chiefly on the upper portions of most of the branches, short, petiolate, or oblong-lanceolate, acute and submucronate, rather coriaceous, dark full-green above, glabrous,

July 1st, 1858.

and wholly destitute of scales; very glaucous beneath, and, as already observed, mealy with copious, orbicular, peltate but sessile *scales*. *Flowers* axillary from the upper and more crowded leaves, nearly sessile, one or sometimes two in each axil, these when fully expanded forming a leafy *head* of flowers of a very delicate rose-colour; and each individual flower is surrounded by large, broad, oval, imbricated, coloured *bracteas*. *Calyx* short, cup-shaped, with five, obtuse, rounded teeth or lobes; the upper half scaly at the back, the margin sometimes ciliated. *Corolla* with the *tube* funnel-shaped, slightly villous on the upper side; *limb* of five, spreading, ovate *segments*. *Stamens* generally ten, nearly straight. *Filaments* hairy at the base. *Anthers* oblong, opening by two large pores. *Ovary* oval. *Style* a little thickened upwards. *Stigma* with five short points.

Fig. 1. Portion of the under side of a leaf. 2. Stamen. 3. Calyx and pistil:—*magnified*. 4. Capsule burst, *nat. size*.

5061.

Tab. 5061.

POLYGONATUM punctatum.

Spotted-stalked Solomon's-seal.

Nat. Ord. Smilacineæ.—Hexandria Monogynia.

Gen. Char. (*Vide supra*, Tab. 5049.)

Polygonatum *punctatum*; glabrum, caule angulato maculato, foliis subdistichis carnosis ovato-lanceolatis obsolete striatis obtuse subacuminatis sessilibus, pedunculis axillaribus bifloris, floribus erectiusculis, perianthio clavato-cylindraceo, ore contracto, limbi lobis subpatentibus ovato-rotundatis alternatim minoribus, filamentis erectis glabris.

Polygonatum punctatum. *Royle, Himal. Fl. v.* 1. *p.* 38. *Kunth, Enum. Plant. v.* 5. *p.* 142.

Convallaria punctata. *Wall. Cat. n.* 5133.

We have lately figured one Indian species of *Polygonatum*, viz. *Polygonatum roseum* (see our Tab. 5049), and we have now to offer another rare Indian species of the same genus. Dr. Wallich, its author, gives it as an inhabitant of Nepal, where Dr. Hooker also found it at a later period, as well as at Sikkim, at an elevation of 7,000 to 11,000 feet above the sea. Our fine flowering specimens were communicated by Mr. Nuttall, from the open ground of his garden at Nutgrove, Rainhill, Lancashire, in April, 1858, having been introduced to his collection by his nephew Mr. Booth, from Bhotan. This species is not described (only named) by Wallich and Royle; and Kunth has certainly erred in describing the leaves as opposite, for ours are clearly alternate, in which respect it differs remarkably from the much better-known *Polygonatum oppositifolium*, Wall.

Descr. *Root* white, thick, tuberous, sending down stout, fleshy *fibres*, and often truncated or præmorse at the end, as in other species of the genus, a circumstance that has given rise to the English generic name of "*Solomon's-seal.*" From this tuber one or more simple *stems* arise, which are erect, about as thick as a goosequill, sheathed at the base with a few, large, imbri-

July 1st, 1858.

cating, thin, membranaceous *scales;* the lower portion leafless, throughout multangular, green, elegantly spotted with brown. *Leaves* alternate, scarcely distichous, approximate, spreading, ovato-lanceolate, sessile, obtusely acuminated, thick and fleshy, obsoletely striated, more distinctly when dry, glabrous as in every part of the plant. *Peduncles* short, erect, solitary, axillary from almost every leaf, bearing generally two, erect or slightly drooping *flowers,* about half an inch long, clavato-cylindraceous, with six furrows, green above, the rest white, spotted with lilac; the mouth contracted; the *limb* of six, moderately spreading, short, ovato-rotundate *lobes,* the three inner ones smaller. *Stamens* quite included. *Filaments* erect, glabrous. *Ovary* broad-ovate, spotted. *Style* short, thick. *Stigma* three-lobed, papillose.

Fig. 1. Flower-stalk and one flower. 2. Pistil:—*magnified.*

5062

5062.

W Fitch del et lith

Vincent Brooks Imp.

Tab. 5062.

THYRSACANTHUS Indicus.

Indian Thyrsacanthus.

Nat. Ord. Acanthaceæ.—Diandria Monogynia.

Gen. Char. (*Vide supra*, Tab. 4378.).

Thyrsacanthus *Indicus;* ramis tetragonis angulis lævibus, foliis oblongo-lanceolatis glabris acuminatis basi attenuatis in petiolum brevem decurrentibus, racemis axillaribus brevibus in racemum terminalem plus minus thyrsoideum subsecundiflorum abeuntibus, corollæ subbilabiatæ laciniis brevibus, filamentis sterilibus rectis. *Nees.*

Thyrsacanthus Indicus. *Nees, in De Cand. Prodr. v.* 2. *p.* 325.

A pretty Acanthaceous plant, but wanting in the richly-coloured flowers of *Thyrs. nitidus, Th. strictus* (see our Tab. 4378), *Th. bracteolatus* (see our Tab. 4441), and some of the other species of the genus, very few of which are known by figure. The present is taken up in De Candolle's 'Prodromus' by the late Nees von Esenbeck, entirely from specimens in the Hookerian Herbarium derived from Assam (*Mrs. Mack, Griffith, Hooker*) and from Khasya (*Griffith, Hooker*). From seeds sent from Bhotan by Mr. Booth, our plants were raised by Mr. Nuttall, and they flowered for the first time, in a warm stove, in April, 1858.

Descr. A shrubby plant with the young shoots only herbaceous. *Stem* and *branches* tetragonal, angles rather acute, smooth. *Leaves* opposite, about three inches long, oblong-lanceolate, pinnato-veined, acuminated, entire, dark-green, tapering gradually at the base into a short *petiole*. *Thyrsus* terminal in our plant. *Peduncles* and *pedicels* bracteated. *Calyx* deeply quinquefid; the segments equal, erect. *Corolla* infundibuliform, the mouth oblique; colour white, with a few purple lines. *Limb* obscurely two-lipped, segments ovate, patenti-reflexed. *Stamens* inserted at the top of the narrow tube, four, erect, didynamous;

two fertile, with large, linear, oblong, acute, purple *anthers;* shorter ones with abortive anthers; *filaments* of both kinds glandular. *Ovary* oblong-ovate, seated upon a large fleshy *disc.* *Style* glandular at the base, as long as the perfect stamens. *Stigma* bifid, the segments subulate.

Fig. 1. Base of the corolla, with stamens. 2. Pistil:—*magnified.*

5063.
1.
2.
3.
4.
5.
W. Fitch del. et lith.
Vincent Brooks Imp.

Tab. 5063.

INDIGOFERA DECORA.

Comely Indigo-plant.

Nat. Ord. Leguminosæ.—Diadelphia Decandria.

Gen. Char. Calyx quinquefidus, lobis acutis. *Vexillum* rotundatum, emarginatum. *Carina* utrinque calcare subulato notata, demum sæpe elastice deflexa. *Stamina* diadelpha. *Stylus* filiformis, glaber. *Legumen* teretiusculum aut planum aut tetragonum, polyspermum, bivalve, rarius oligospermum, ovatum, imo monospermum, subglobosum. *Semina* ovata, utrinque truncata, isthmis cellulosis sæpe disjuncta.—Herbæ *aut* suffrutices; stipulæ *a petiolo distinctæ, parvæ.* Pedunculi *axillares.* Flores *racemosi, purpurei cærulei aut albi.* Folia *nunc simplicia (pinnata ad impar reducta), impari-pinnata aut digitata,* foliolis *sæpe basi stipellatis.* Pili *nunc omnes, nunc plerique strigosi, centro adfixi, adpressi. De Cand.*

Indigofera *decora;* fruticosa glabra glaucescens, foliis pinnatis, petiolis 2–5-jugis exacte ovatis obtusis cum mucrone subtus pilis sparsis peltatis obsitis, racemis elongatis densis folia subæquantibus, calyce hemisphærico quinquedentato, carinæ margine superiore villoso. *Lindl.*

Indigofera decora. *Lindl. in Journ. of Hort. Soc. v.* 1. *p.* 68. *Bot. Reg. v.* 32. *t.* 22.

A most lovely and ornamental greenhouse plant, by no means so generally seen in our collections as it deserves to be; a native of China, and cultivated in the gardens of Shanghai, whence Mr. Fortune introduced it to the Horticultural Society of London. It flowers early in the season, and a cool greenhouse is rendered quite gay with its blossoms, which are of a lively pink and rose-colour, arranged in long, erect racemes; add to which the leaves are pinnated and of the most delicate green.

Descr. A *shrub*, or small but straggling *bush*, the *branches* needing support. Indeed it does best trailed against the wall, or on a rafter, treated as a half-climber. *Branches* slender, terete, tinged with red. *Leaves* a span long, pinnated, with an odd one. *Pinnæ* six to eight pairs, broad lanceolate, generally drooping, slightly villous beneath, with hairs fixed by the middle; a pair of distinct *stipules* at the base of the petioles, and lesser ones at the base of the short petiolules. *Racemes* elongated, axillary, solitary, as long as or longer than the leaves, bearing numerous, patent or deflexed, pink and rose-coloured *flowers*, almost an inch long. *Calyx* short, cup-shaped, five-toothed, spreading. *Standard* oblong, rather obtuse, streaked with a horse-shoe band near the base, strict (not patent or reflexed). *Alæ* linear-lanceolate or spathulate, ciliated. *Carina* oblong-lanceolate, very acute, ciliated at the upper edge. *Stamens* diadelphous. *Anthers* ovate, with a tuft or pencil of hairs at the apex. *Ovary* linear-cylindrical. *Style* subulate. *Stigma* small, capitate.

Fig. 1. Standard. 2. One of the wings. 3. Keel. 4. Calyx and stamens. 5. Pistil:—*magnified*.

W Fitch del et lith. Vincent Brooks Imp.

Tab. 5064.

AZALEA ovata.

Ovate-leaved Chinese Azalea.

Nat. Ord. Ericeæ.—Pentandria Monogynia.

Gen. Char. (*Vide supra*, Tab. 4726.)

Azalea *ovata;* glaberrima, foliis coriaceis petiolatis ovatis ovato-subcordatisve acutis emarginatisve, pedunculis glanduloso-hispidis unifloris ex axillis supremis, floribus 5-andris, sepalis ovatis membranaceis glabris subciliatis, corolla rotata ad basin fere 5-partita, laciniis obovatis oblongisve obtusis, filamentis infra medium pilosis, ovario glanduloso.

Var. α; floribus pallide purpureis. (Tab. Nostr. 5064.)

Var. β; floribus pallide roseis.

Azalea ovata. *Lindl. in Hort. Soc. Journ. v.* 1. *p.* 149. *Fortune in Hort. Soc. Journ. v.* 2. *p.* 126. *t.* 2.

Var. γ; floribus albis.

Azalea myrtifolia. *Champion in Hook. Bot. Mag. sub t.* 4609. *Benth. Flor. Hongkong. in Kew Journ. Bot. v.* 4. *p.* 298.

A very pretty little shrub, introduced from Northern China by Mr. Fortune, and first described by Dr. Lindley, from both a white- and pale-pink-flowered variety, in 1844. Our specimens were received from the garden of the Horticultural Society, in June, 1858. The same species was afterwards found in Hongkong by the late Captain Champion, and, from differing in some points from Lindley's description, he named it *A. myrtifolia*.

Descr. A half-hardy shrub or small tree, with few small shining green leaves towards the tips of the short branches, and axillary, solitary, peduncled flowers. *Leaves* about an inch long, ovate or ovate-cordate, acuminate or emarginate, glabrous. *Peduncles* short, glanduloso-pubescent. *Calyx-lobes* membranous, oblong, blunt, subciliated. *Flowers* pale-purple, upper lobe of corolla speckled with dark-purple. *Corolla* rotate, with broad lobes. *Stamens* five, with filaments hairy below the middle. *Ovary* glandular, five-celled.—*J. D. H.*

Fig. 1. Stamen. 2. Calyx and pistil. 3. Ovary. 4. Transverse section of ditto:—*all magnified.*

August 1st, 1858.

W. Fitch del. et lith.

Vincent Brooks Imp.

Tab. 5065.

RHODODENDRON Griffithianum, *Wight*; var. *Aucklandii*.

Lord Auckland's Rhododendron.

Nat. Ord. Ericeæ.—Decandria Monogynia.

Gen. Char. (*Vide supra*, Tab. 4336.)

Rhododendron *Griffithianum*; glaberrimum, foliis sublonge petiolatis lineari-oblongis ovato-oblongisve utrinque acutis v. basi subcordatis subtus pallidis, floribus corymbosis, calyce lato disciformi margine crenato v. 5-lobo, corolla campanulata 5-loba, lobis rotundatis bifidis, staminibus sub-16, antheris parvis, ovario sub-12-loculari glanduloso, capsula brevi obtusa.

Var. α; foliis 4-pollicaribus utrinque acutis, floribus 3 poll. latis.

Rhododendron Griffithianum. *Wight, Ic. Plant. Ind. Or. v.* 4. *t.* 1203. *Hook. fil. in Journ. Hort. Soc. v.* 7. *pp.* 77, 93.

Var. β; foliis 6–12-pollicaribus basi obtusis cordatisve, floribus 6–7 poll. latis.

Rhododendron Aucklandii. *Hook. fil. Sikkim Rhod. t.* 11.

This magnificent plant, which from the great expanse of its snowy-white corollas is in some respects the finest of the genus, was introduced by Dr. Hooker from the Sikkim Himalaya in 1849, and flowered at the nursery of Mr. Gaines, at Wandsworth, in May of the present year. It was originally found in Bhotan by Mr. Griffith, where specimens are however so inferior, both in foliage and flowers, to the Sikkim ones, that the figure given of them by Dr. Wight in his invaluable 'Icones' can scarcely be recognized as belonging to the same species. In Sikkim, however, two states of the species occur, one with much smaller flowers than the other, and it was at first doubted by Dr. Hooker, whether the gigantic-flowered state figured here and in his 'Sikkim Rhododendrons,' was not a sterile form. Such, however, appears not to be the case, for Mr. Gaines's plant produced abundance of pollen, and his specimen differs

August 1st, 1858.

in no respect from Dr. Hooker's plate, except in the paler anthers, greener petioles, and in wanting the rose-coloured hue and spots on the calyx.

DESCR. A *shrub*, four to eight feet high, branching from the base. *Leaves* spreading, six to twelve inches long, linear-oblong, acute or acuminate, subcordate at the base, of a fine bright-green edged with pale-yellow, coriaceous and firm. *Flowers* four to six, in terminal corymbose racemes, long-peduncled, very large, sometimes seven inches across. *Calyx* discoid, coriaceous, obscurely lobed. *Corolla* campanulate, with a short tube and open limb, five-lobed; *lobes* bifid. *Stamens* about sixteen, with glabrous filaments and small anthers. *Ovary* glandular, about twelve-celled. *Capsule* short, blunt, woody.

Fig. 1. Stamen. 2. Calyx and pistil. 3. Transverse section of ovary:—*all magnified*.

5066.

W Fitch del et lith.

Vincent Brooks Imp.

TAB. 5066.

SAXIFRAGA PURPURASCENS.

Purple Himalayan Saxifrage.

Nat. Ord. SAXIFRAGEÆ.—DECANDRIA DIGYNIA.

Gen. Char. (*Vide supra*, TAB. 4915.)

SAXIFRAGA (§ Bergenia) *purpurascens;* foliis obovato-rotundatis integerrimis eciliatis glaberrimis, panicula subcorymbosa scapoque purpureo pubescenti-glanduloso, floribus omnibus nutantibus, calyce profunde 5-lobo, petalis longe late unguiculatis purpureis.

SAXIFRAGA purpurascens. *Hook. fil. et Thoms. in Linn. Soc. Journ. Bot. v.* 2. *p.* 61.

This beautiful and hardy species was raised at Kew from seeds sent by Dr. Hooker from the temperate regions of the Sikkim Himalaya, where it was discovered growing in wet places, at an elevation of 10,000 to 14,000 feet. Though closely allied to the Himalayan *S. ligulata,* Wall. (Bot. Mag. t. 3406), *S. ciliata,* Royle (Bot. Mag. t. 4915), and the Siberian *S. crassifolia,* L. (Bot. Mag. t. 196), it is extremely different from, and far more beautiful than, any of those species; nothing, indeed, can exceed the bright glossy green of its leaves, which are elegantly margined with red, or the deep, bright, vinous red-purple of its scape and inflorescence.

DESCR. A hardy perennial, with a stout, short, branching, prostrate rootstock. *Leaves* coriaceous, on short, thick, red petioles; *blade* rounded, obovate, blunt at both ends, bright glossy green above, paler below, with red midrib and margins. *Scape* very stout, six to eight inches high, deep red-purple, covered, as is the inflorescence, with a short, glandular pubescence. *Flowers* few in native specimens, more numerous and larger in cultivated ones, forming a dense, branched, subcorymbose panicle, all drooping. *Calyx* deeply five-lobed, lobes blunt. *Petals* forming a campanulate corolla, broadly spathulate. *Ovaries* generally two.—*J. D. H.*

Fig. 1. Pistil, *magnified.*

AUGUST 1ST, 1858.

Vincent Brooks Imp

Tab. 5067.

ISMELIA Broussonetii.

Broussonet's Ismelia.

Nat. Ord. Compositæ.—Syngenesia Superflua.

Gen. Char. Capitulum multiflorum, heterogamum; *floribus radii* uniserialibus, fœmineis fertilibus lingulatis 8–10- (imo in *I. carinata* 12–14-) striatis, apice rotundatis vel lævissime et obsolete tridentatis (in *I. carinata* quandoque profunde emarginatis); *tubo* granulato hirto, pilis sæpe glanduliferis, intime cum achenio concreto (vel in *I. carinata* articulatim juncto); *floribus disci* innumeris, hermaphroditis, tubulosis, quinquedentatis, punctis resinosis vel pilis glanduliferis obsitis. *Involucrum* hemisphæricum, imbricatum; *squamis* apice in appendicem magnam scariosam expansis. *Receptaculum* nudum, elongato- vel depresso-conicum (vel in *I. carinata* plano-convexum). *Achenia* difformia, concoloria; *radii* fertilia, crassa, turbinato-triangulari, alata, alis cum pappo coroniformi, margine scarioso, quandoque rudimentario (imo in *I. Broussonetii* tantum dentibus paucis robustis parte interiore); *disci* pleraque sterilia, compressiuscula, ancipitia, bialata, alis lateralibus cum pappo coroniformi margine scariosis.—Suffrutices *Canarienses et Mauritanici, glabri vel hirti, foliosi, ramosi;* foliis *pinnatifidis, in petiolum integrum vel dentatum angustatis;* pedunculis *elongatis*, radio *albo*, disco *flavo* (in *I. carinata* radio *albo-flavescente*, disco *atro-purpureo*). *C. H. Schultz Bipont.*

Ismelia *Broussonetii;* suffruticulus spithamæo-pedalis glaber vel hirtus, foliis obovato-oblongis profunde pinnatifidis in petiolum dentatum, acheniis disci striato-costatis bialatis. *C. H. Schultz.*

Ismelia Broussonetii. *C. H. Schultz Bipont. in Webb, Phytogr. Canar. p.* 274. *t.* 95. *f.* 3, 5, *and* 9 (Argyranthemum pinnatifidum, *Webb, on plate*). *Walp. Repert. Bot. v.* 6. *p.* 202.

Chrysanthemum pinnatifidum. *Brousson. Herb.* (*fide Webb*).

Chrysanthemum Broussonetii. *Balbis, Cat. H. Taur.* (1850), *p.* 20. *De Cand. Prodr. v.* 6. *p.* 66.

Pyrethrum Broussonetii. *Choisy in Buch. Canar. p.* 149. *Spreng. Syst. Veget. v.* 3. *p.* 584.

Pyrethrum adauctum. *Link in Buch. Canar.* 19–181 (*excl. loco natali 'Madera,' Webb*).

This Canarian plant, although belonging to the "Ox-eye" group of *Compositæ*, which we are too much in the habit of looking upon as coarse weeds, is really a handsome plant, new to our gardens, till we raised it from seeds at Kew, sent to us by M. Bourgeau, and which will probably prove hardy, though at present we have kept it in a cool greenhouse. It is peculiar to the Canary Islands, growing in the "Laurel region" in the mountain-ranges, elev. about 3000 feet above the sea-level. As a genus it has vacillated between *Pyrethrum* and *Chrysanthemum*; but, if our figures be correct and Mr. Webb's correct also, the characters derived from the wings and pappus of the achenia are not wholly to be depended upon. In the month of May the flowers had quite a striking appearance in a conservatory.

Descr. *Plant* erect or ascending, branched, shrubby at the base, glabrous, two to three feet high: a span to a foot in its native country, so that the species seems to be greatly improved by cultivation. *Stem* and *branches* striated, quite herbaceous above. *Leaves* distant, ovate in circumscription, the superior ones obovate, all deeply, nearly to the costa, pinnatifid; the *segments* lanceolate, often again pinnatifid and toothed, decurrent to the base of the petiole, which is dentato-pinnatifid. *Peduncles* elongated, incrassated upwards. *Involucre* of several green, ovate *scales*, with broad brown scarious margins. *Flowers* three inches across. *Ray* pale-lilac, tinged with yellow at the base. *Disc* at first dark-purple, golden-yellow when the florets are fully expanded.

Fig. 1. Floret of the ray. 2. Floret of the disc:—*magnified*.

Tab. 5068.

CAMPANULA strigosa.

Strigose Bell-flower.

Nat. Ord. Campanulaceæ.—Pentandria Monogynia.

Gen. Char. Calyx 5-fidus. *Corolla* apice 5-loba vel 5-fida, sæpius campanulata. *Stamina* 5, libera, filamentis basi latis et membranaceis. *Stylus* in præfloratione pilis collectoribus (excepta ima basi) tectus. *Stigmata* 3 vel 5, filiformia. *Capsula* 3-locularis, *valvis* 3–5 lateraliter dehiscens. *Semina* ovata complanata vel ovoidea.—Herbæ *sæpius perennes, nunc humiles et humifusæ, nunc* 2–3-*pedales, erectæ, multifloræ;* foliis *radicalibus, sæpius forma diversis;* floribus *terminalibus vel axillaribus. Omnes in hemisphærio boreali. De Cand.*

Campanula (§ Medium) *strigosa;* annua erecta flexuosa parce dichotomo-ramosa, foliis oblongo-ovatis integerrimis sessilibus, floribus solitariis inter ramos dichotomos vel folio oppositis, lobis calycinis apice longe apice subulatis basi latis erectis corolla tubuloso-campanulata subbrevioribus (calycis) appendicibus insigniter deflexis ovatis ovarium totum tegentibus.

Campanula strigosa. "*Russel, Descr. of Alep.*" (*De Cand.*). *Alph. De Cand. Monogr. Campan. p.* 236. *Vahl, Symbol. v.* 8. *p.* 34. *Ræm. et Sch. Syst. Veget. v.* 5. *p.* 142 (*et C. Russeliana, R. et S.*). *De Cand. Prodr. v.* 7. *p.* 462.

Native of Syria, especially about Aleppo, where, according to De Candolle, it was first detected and named by Russel; and it has since been gathered by Labillardière and Aucher-Éloy, and in the Taurus by Kotschy. Balansa collected it in Cilicia, and seeds have been communicated to us by Professor Fenzl from the Imperial Botanic Garden of Vienna. At present we have only reared it in a pot in a cool frame, and its bright flowers give a very gay appearance to a cluster of plants. There can be little doubt that it would prove hardy enough for a border annual, and perhaps for bedding out. Even in a pot it has continued flowering for a month, without any abatement in beauty.

Descr. Herbaceous, annual, everywhere, but especially the peduncles and calyces, strigose with white, pellucid, patent *hairs. Stems* erect, flexuose, four to five inches high, terete, patentihispid, dichotomous at the summit only. *Leaves* remote, alternate, ciliate, oblong-ovate, sessile, patent or reflexed, quite entire at the margin. *Peduncles* terminal or in the axil of a fork, rarely lateral, single-flowered. *Calyx* very large in proportion to the flower, and very curious in structure, for at first sight it appears to have an insertion inferior to the ovary: the free portion of the calyx is five-parted; *segments* ovate, hispid, terminated by a subulate spreading apex, the base of each descends as it were, and forms two *ears* or *appendages*, which quite conceal the ovary, which is small and turbinate. *Corolla* campanulato-infundibuliform; the *tube* yellowish-white, a little longer than the calyx. *Stamens*, with the *filaments*, broad oval, bifid at the apex, and between the two lobes the linear *anther* is inserted. *Style* larger than the stamens, clavate. *Stigmas* three short lobes.

Fig. 1. Flower deprived of the corolla. 2. The same, with the lobes of the calyx removed:—*magnified*.

5069

Tab. 5069.

GUSTAVIA insignis.

Showy Gustavia.

Nat. Ord. Myrtaceæ: Tribe Barringtonieæ.—Monadelphia Polyandria.

Gen. Char. Calycis tubus turbinatus, limbus integer aut 4–6–8-lobus. *Petala* 4–6–8, ovalia, subæqualia. *Stamina* numerosa, basi monadelphia unguibusque petalorum subadnata. *Ovarium* 4–6-loculare, loculis polyspermis. *Stylus* brevis. *Stigma* obtusum. *Capsula* ovata aut subglobosa, 3–6-locularis, coriacea, calycis vestigio umbilicata. *Semina* in quoque loculo pauca ovata, membrana coriacea vestita, *funiculo* longo plicato columnæ centrali affixo suspensa. *Embryo* carnosus. *Cotyledones* 2, magnæ, subæquales, extus convexæ, intus planæ. *Radicula* obtusa, vix prominens.—Arbores; folia *alterna, magna, impunctata, serrata aut integerrima, glabra.* Racemi *terminales, pauciflori.* Flores *bracteati, albi, speciosi. De Cand.*

Gustavia *insignis;* floribus 6-petalis, calyce 6-lobo, lobis rotundatis pedunculoque glaberrimo, ovario aptero, foliis obovato-lanceolatis acuminatis spinuloso-serratis basi attenuatis, bracteis floralibus ad basin ovarii.

Gustavia insignis. *Linden Cat.* 1855 (*name only*).

Eight species of the fine tropical American genus *Gustavia* are defined by De Candolle in the 'Prodromus,' and Mr. Bentham has since added a ninth, but none of these sufficiently accord with the present plant to justify me in referring it to any one of them; so that if those species are accurately characterized, and if the characters are constant, our plant must be new. The most nearly allied species are: (1) *G. angusta*, L., which has eight petals and a truncated calyx; (2) *G. speciosa*, De Cand. (*Pirigara speciosa*, H. B. K.), with a nearly entire calyx, a tomentose ovary and peduncles, and entire leaves; and (3) *G. urceolata*, Poir., with the calyx entire. *G. angusta* and *G. speciosa* have, further, the pair of bracteas remote from the flower, whereas in our plant they are appressed to the base of the ovary. In other respects this has the most perfect resemblance to *G. urceolata*, the figure and description of which are given in the 'Mém. du Museum,' v. 13, p. 156, t. 5. Here however we have a distinct, five-lobed calyx, and I think it safer to adopt the name by which it is circulated from the Belgian gardens, and printed (without a word of description or remark) in Linden's Catalogue of 1855. It is probably a native of Columbia or Guiana; and is certainly possessed of great beauty both in the foliage and in the great, *Clusia*-like flower. It blossomed with us in June, 1858.

DESCR. With us, *Gustavia insignis* constitutes a *shrub* three or four feet high, a good deal branched. *Leaves* a span and more long, dark-green, glossy, obovato-lanceolate, acuminated at the point, much attenuated at the base, and sessile or nearly so; *veins* pinnated, rather strong: the margin towards the apex coarsely and irregularly spinuloso-serrated, the base and apex entire. *Peduncles* from the axils of the upper leaves, in our plant a solitary and single flower (probably sometimes racemose and few-flowered), stout, glabrous, terete, each two to four inches long, with a few small, broad, ovate bracts at the base, and two opposite ones at the base of the ovary. *Calyx* (with its inferior ovary) urceolate, almost like that of the Pomegranate, the *tube* turbinate, the *limb* of six, broad-ovate or rounded lobes, at first (in bud) erect, at length spreading. *Corolla* very large, five to six inches in diameter. *Petals* in our specimens six, broadly obovate, cream-white, concave, spreading, externally tinged with rose-colour. *Stamens* extremely numerous, in many series, combined at the base only, hence monadelphous, arising as it were from a fleshy ring. *Filaments* rose-colour towards the apex, and there a little clavate. *Anthers* orange-colour, articulated on the apex of the filament, two-celled. *Ovary* circular, turbinate, incorporated with the tube of the calyx, expanded and depressed at the top. *Stigma* very small, short, crowned by a minute four-lobed *stigma*.

Fig. 1. Portion of the staminal tube, with filaments and anthers, *magnified*. 2. Ovary and calyx. 3. Vertical section of ovary and calyx. 4. Transverse section of ovary, showing the four cells and numerous ovules:—*nat. size*.

5070

W. Fitch del et lith

Vincent Brooks Imp.

Tab. 5070.

GESNERIA Donklarii.

Donklar's Gesneria.

Nat. Ord. Gesneriaceæ.—Didynamia Gymnospermia.

Gen. Char. (*Vide supra*, Tab. 4217.)

Gesneria *Donklarii;* elata ubique velutino-pubescens, foliis inferioribus amplis cordato-rotundatis acutis duplicato-crenatis, superioribus sensim minoribus ovatis acutis serratis omnibus petiolatis reticulatim venosis subtus purpureis, paniculis pyramidatis multifloris, pedunculis plerisque trifloris, pedicellis elongatis, floribus nutantibus, segmentis calycinis lanceolato-subulatis patentibus, corollæ (coccineæ) tubo elongato paulululum curvato-inflatoque, limbo subregulari 5-lobo fauce aperta, staminibus styloque inclusis.

Gesneria Donklarii. *Hort.*

One of the handsomest of Gesneriaceous plants now in cultivation in our stoves. We are enabled to figure this plant from the rich collection of Messrs. Veitch and Son's Nurseries of Exeter and Chelsea, where it flowered in June of the present year. It is probably a native of Columbia, a region so rich in species of this genus, but at present we only know the plant in a state of cultivation. If the colours of the flowers are not so bright as those of many species of the genus, their size, and the fine velvety foliage, dark-green on the upper surface, purple beneath, amply compensate for that imperfection.

Descr. *Plant* a foot and a half to two feet high in its perfect flowering state, and then forming a pyramidal outline; the *leaves* below very large, gradually smaller upwards, and they become converted into bracts at the bases of the pseudo-whorls of the panicle. *Stem* stout, dark-purple throughout. *Lower leaves* a span long, rotundate- or orbicular-cordate, acute, the margin doubly crenate; upper ones gradually smaller, ovate, slightly acuminate, rather coarsely serrated: all of them downy and velutinous, strongly reticulato-venose, petiolate, dark uniform green above, purple beneath. *Panicle* terminal, large, erect, many-flowered; *peduncles*, the lower ones at least, bearing three flowers on long erecto-patent, dark-purple, downy *pedicels*, bracteated at the base. *Flowers* large, drooping. *Calyx* purple, of five, deep, subulate *segments,* closing upon the ovary when the corolla has fallen. *Corolla* more than two inches long, red, but of rather a dull hue; the *tube* very slightly curved and moderately inflated, gibbous at the base above; *limb* spreading, a little oblique, five-lobed, lobes rounded, equal or nearly so; the mouth of the tube is open, yellow within. *Stamens* included. *Pistil* also included. *Ovary* ovate, villous, with two erect, appressed, oblong-ovate, fleshy glands at the base. *Style* and *stigma* as in the genus.

Fig. 1. Pistil. 2. Ovary, showing the two glands:—*magnified.*

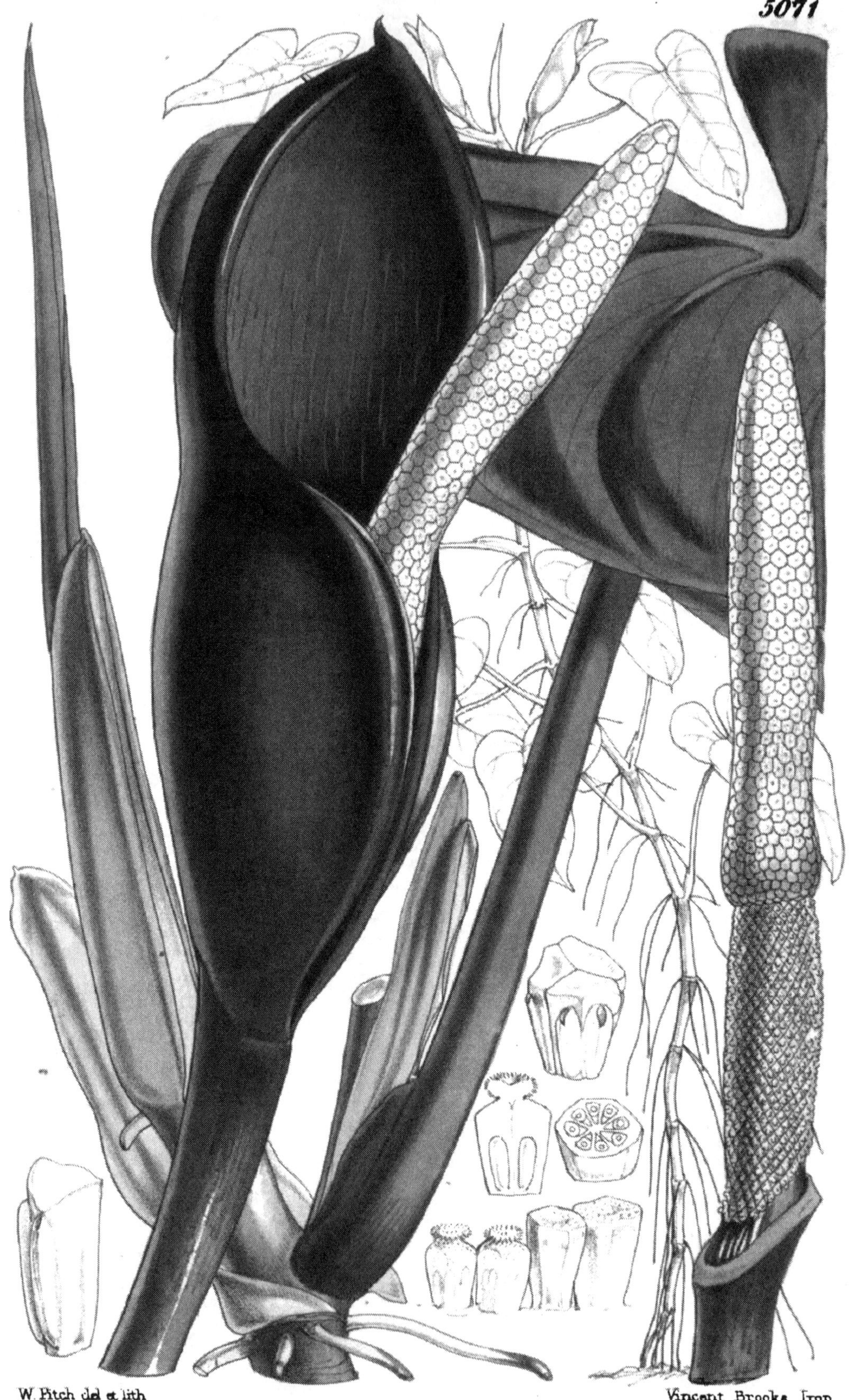

W. Fitch del et lith

Vincent Brooks Imp

Tab. 5071.

PHILODENDRON ERUBESCENS.

Red-purple Philodendron.

Nat. Ord. Aroideæ.—Monœcia Polyandria.

Gen. Char. *Spatha* tota persistens, post florescentiam reclusa. *Spadix* dense obsitus, appendice carens. *Antheræ* singuli floris liberæ. *Ovarium* multi- (5–15-) loculare; *loculis* pluriovulatis; *ovulis* axi affixis, erectis.—Plantæ *Americanæ tropicæ*, succo *decolori*, rhizomate *in caulem elongatum scandentem v. arborescentem mutato*, foliis *remotis*, vaginis *petiolaribus brevissimis*, stipularibus *elongatis deciduis folio oppositis*. *Schott.*

Philodendron *erubescens*; elata scandens, caule subsimplici ad nodos copiose radicante, foliis pedalibus et ultra sagittato-cordatis acutis utrinque nitidis viridibus subtus pallide purpurascentibus vel cupreis, venis superne immersis, petiolo tereti folii longitudine, pedunculis brevibus subterminalibus, spatha cucullato-cymbiformi obtusa cum mucronulo carnoso firma extus atro-purpurascente intus kermesina, spadice spathæ longitudine crasso dimidio inferiore ovariis tecto, apice staminigero medio staminodiis tecto.

Philodendron erubescens. "*C. Koch* (*App.* 1854, *p.* 6)." *Schott, Syn. Aroid.* 1. *p.* 88.

Aroideous plants are not so much cultivated as they deserve, if the varied forms, the noble foliage, the peculiar inflorescence, with its occasional rich colouring and very often delicious fragrance be considered. They constitute a very striking feature in tropical forests, and one stove at Kew is mainly devoted to a considerable collection of them. Amongst these, the present species stands conspicuous, with its glossy leaves, dark-purple boat-shaped spathas, crimson within, and their white columnar spadices. We are indebted for the species of *Philodendron* here figured to the most learned of botanists in this family of plants, Dr. Schott; and receiving it with that name, we cannot doubt its being the true *P. erubescens* of Koch and Schott (ll: cc.), otherwise, the foliage being alone described, I should scarcely have ventured to consider it identical. But indeed, without good figures, it is very difficult to determine the genera and species of *Aroideæ*. The present is certainly nearly allied to *Arum grandifolium*, Jacq. (Hort. Schœnbr. t. 189; Hook. Bot. Mag. t. 3345=*Philodendron Hookeri*, Schott), differing however totally in the colour of the spatha, white or cream-colour in *P. grandifolium*. The native country is not known, probably the Caracas.

Descr. *Stem* elongated, stout, flexuose, climbing, jointed, rooting at almost every joint; the lower roots very much lengthened and penetrating into the ground; the others slightly attach themselves to decayed wood, which is placed to afford support to the plant. *Leaves* distant, alternate, large, a foot or more long, on terete *petioles* of about the same length, with purple sheaths at the base. The blade or *lamina* of the leaf is between cordate and sagittate, the *lobes* somewhat spreading, blunt; glossy on both sides, beneath of a coppery colour. The *veins* are sunk in the upper side of the leaf, slightly prominent beneath. *Stipule* long, sheathing, palish-purple, more or less acuminated. *Peduncle* opposite the leaves, with a large sheathing *bract* or stipule at the base, purple-green. *Spatha* large, conspicuous by its size and colour, boat-shaped, thick and fleshy, convolute, slightly contracted above the middle, the lower half and more convolute, the apex blunt, with a mucro; the *colour*, without, deep blackish-purple, scarlet within. *Spadix* equal in length to the spatha, stout, obtuse, white or cream-colour; the lower half or nearly so is clothed with pistils; a circle of sessile *anthers* occupies the middle portion, and the rest of the clavate upper half is clothed with peltate stamens.

Our figures represent an entire plant on a very reduced scale, together with a portion of a leaf and spadix and spatha, *nat. size*. Fig. 1. Spadix, also *nat. size*. 2. Pistils. 3. Staminodia. 4. Ovary, cut through vertically. 5. One cut through transversely. 6. Stamens. 7. Single stamen, with two-celled anthers:—*magnified*.

5072.

W. Fitch, del. et lith.

Vincent Brooks Imp.

TAB. 5072.

CŒLOGYNE SCHILLERIANA.

Schiller's Cœlogyne.

Nat. Ord. ORCHIDEÆ—GYNANDRIA MONANDRIA

Gen. Char. (*Vide supra*, TAB. 5001.)

CŒLOGYNE (Pleione) *Schilleriana;* labelli tripartiti partitionibus posticis semiovatis antice acutangulis, partitione media a basi constricta transverse oblonga maxima marginibus revoluta, apice emarginata, limbo denticulato, carinis ternis per discum ad ortum partitionis mediæ. *Reichb. fil.*

CŒLOGYNE Schilleriana. *Reichb. fil. in Berliner Allgem. Gartenzeitung, June* 12*th*, 1858.

Of this tropical Asiatic genus, no less than forty-three species are described by Dr. Lindley in the fifth part of his valuable 'Folia Orchidacea,' published in 1853. Among the additions that have been since made is the present one from Moulmein, introduced by Messrs. Veitch and Son, of the Exeter and Chelsea Nurseries, through their collector, Mr. Thomas Lobb. It flowered in June; 1858. I am indebted to Dr. Lindley for the name of this plant, and for the extract of the specific character and remarks of Dr. Reichenbach, from a publication to which I have not myself ready access.

DESCR. *Pseudobulbs* small or bottle-shaped, clustered, truncated when old from the falling away of the former years' foliage. New plants form by the side of the old bulbs, at first scarcely exhibiting an appearance of pseudobulbs; these are fully developed as the plant perfects itself. *Leaves* two, lanceolate, obscurely nerved, between coriaceous and membranaceous, spreading, acute, tapering and narrowed very much into a *petiole* at the base, and there clothed with imbricated, herbaceous *scales*. *Peduncle* arising from between the two leaves and shorter than they, erect, single-flowered (in our specimen). *Flower* large for the size of the plant; its ground colour tawny-yellow, expanded, in perfection at the same time with the leaves. *Sepals* an inch and a half long, very patent, lanceolate, acute. *Petals* much smaller and quite linear, pendent like the two lower sepals. *Labellum* large, porrected, somewhat broad-lyre-shaped, three-lobed, *lateral lobes* oblong, incurved upon the column, middle lobe very large, constricted at the base, nearly orbicular, waved and dentate at the margin, tubercled on the surface, bifid at the apex : the *disc* of the lip has three principal elevated lines extending from the base, beyond the centre, and several transverse, orange-coloured, and the middle lobe blotched and spotted with orange. *Column* semiterete. *Anther-case* conical, obtuse.

Fig. 1. Column and anther. 2. Front view of the labellum. 3. Pollen-masses :—*magnified.*

5073.

W. Fitch, del et lith.

Vincent Brooks, Imp.

Tab. 5073.

ISOTOMA senecioides; var. *subpinnatifida.*

Groundsel-leaved Isotoma; subpinnatifid var.

Nat. Ord. Lobeliaceæ.—Pentandria Monogynia.

Gen. Char. Calyx 5-lobus, tubo turbinato vel elongato. *Corolla* hypocraterimorpha, *tubo* integro, *lobis* calycinis multo longiore, recto vel subincurvo, lobis patentibus æqualibus vel paulo inæqualibus. *Filamenta* staminum tubo corollæ plus minusve adnata. *Antheræ* extra tubum corollæ inter se connatæ, 2 inferioribus apice setaceo-aristatis.—Herbæ *sæpius annuæ*, pedicellis *axillaribus*, floribus *albis roseis vel cæruleis. De Cand.*

Isotoma *senecioides*; subpubescens, caule erecto anguloso, foliis lineari-lanceolatis subdecurrentibus irregulariter pinnatifidis lobis alternatim brevioribus, pedunculis axillaribus erectis gracilibus unifloris folio duplo triplove longioribus, calycis tubo obconico, lobis lineari-acuminatis patentibus tubo corollæ quadruplo brevioribus, laciniis corollæ lanceolatis acutis duplo triplove brevioribus.

Isotoma senecioides. *De Cand. Prodr. v.* 7. *p.* 412.

Lobelia senecioides. *All. Cunn. MSS. Hook. Bot. Mag. t.* 2702.

Isotoma axillaris.. *Lindl. Bot. Reg. t.* 964. *Lodd. Bot. Cab. t.* 1508. *Gaudich. in Freyc. Bot. p.* 455. *t.* 70.

β; foliis subbipinnatifidis. (Tab. Nostr. 5073.)

A very pretty greenhouse plant, native of Bathurst, New South Wales, where it was found by Allan Cunningham, and it was afterwards gathered in the same locality by Mr. Fraser. *Isotoma* is a name given to a section of *Lobelia* by the learned Brown, intended for his *Lobelia hypocrateriformis*, figured by us at Tab. 3075. This section has been adopted by Dr. Lindley as a genus, and to this he has added the *Lobelia senecioides* of Allan Cunningham, of which the plant here figured is a variety, with the leaves more compound, so as to be generally bipinnatifid. This species has a different habit and a different form of corolla from the original *Isotoma*. And with these M. De Candolle has united the Caribean *Lobelia longiflora* of Presl and Willdenow (*Hippobroma longiflora*, G. Don). We have no wish to run counter to such high authority; yet we will observe that the genus does not appear to our eyes to be a natural one, nor sufficiently distinct from *Lobelia*.

September 1st, 1858.

The more usual form of the species having been fully described at our Tab. 2702, we shall refer our readers there, merely observing that in the state here figured the laciniæ of the leaves are longer than in the ordinary form of the plant, and not unfrequently again pinnatifid.

Fig. 1. Pistil and calyx. 2. Column of stamens:—*magnified.*

5074
2
1
W. Fitch, del et lith.
Vincent Brooks, Imp.

Tab. 5074.

ORCHIS foliosa.

Leafy Orchis.

Nat. Ord. Orchideæ.—Gynandria Monogynia.

Gen. Char. Flores galeati. *Sepala* subæqualia; supremum cum petalis in fornicis speciem connivens; lateralia nunc convergentia nunc reflexa. *Petala* erecta, sepalo subæqualia. *Labellum* anticum, calcaratum, integrum v. indivisum, cum basi columnæ connatum. *Anthera* erecta, loculis contiguis parallelis. *Glandulæ* polleniorum 2, distinctæ, cucullo communi (*i. e.* plicatura cucullata stigmatis s. rostelli) inclusæ.—Herbæ *terrestres*, radicibus *tuberculiferis*, foliis *plerisque radicalibus tactu mollibus subsucculentis sæpe maculatis. Lindl.*

Orchis *foliosa;* foliis oblongo-lanceolatis acuminatis laxe vaginantibus, spica oblonga multiflora, sepalis ovatis acutis, labello latiore quam longo obsolete trilobo plano, laciniis lateralibus emarginatis intermedia acuta multo majoribus, calcare pendulo cornuto labello duplo breviore, bracteis herbaceis acuminatis flore sæpe longioribus, tuberculis palmatis. *Lindl.*

Orchis foliosa. *Soland. MSS. in Herb. Banks. Lowe, Primit. Fl. Mader. p.* 13. *Lindley, Bot. Reg. t.* 1701; *Sert. Orchid. t.* 44.

This fine *Orchis* is a good deal allied, it must be confessed, to our *Orchis latifolia*, but nevertheless truly distinct; differing, as Dr. Lindley assures us, in being larger in all its parts, having a distinctly three-lobed, flat lip, instead of a lozenge-shaped convex one, a shorter and more slender spur, and a taller stem. It is a species peculiar to the island of Madeira, and is found, according to the Rev. Mr. Lowe, from whom we possess specimens, in rocky banks of Ribeiro Frio, amongst grass and bushes of *Spartium candicans*, at an elevation upon the hills of 3000 feet. Our roots were sent to us by Mr. Fraser, of the Comely Bank Nursery, Edinburgh, in 1857, and the present individual flowered in a cool greenhouse in 1858. Mr. Lowe gathered one native specimen which measured two feet seven inches in height.

Descr. *Tubers* palmated. *Stem* and *foliage* resembling greatly those of *Orchis latifolia*, spotless. *Bracteas* leafy among the flowers, but generally shorter than they. *Spike* ovate or oblong-ovate, three inches broad, bearing numerous purple flowers. *Sepals* erecto-patent, ovate, obtuse, nearly plane, palish-purple. *Petals* similar in form, but narrower and smaller, nearly erect, dark-purple. *Lip* pendent, very broad, rotundato-cuneate, three-lobed, middle lobe the smallest: the *colour* purple, with darker blotches of the same colour. *Spur* a good deal shorter than the lip, purple, with darker blotches.

Fig. 1. Flower. 2. Column, anther, and base of the lip, with the spur:—*magnified.*

5075.
1.
2.
J Fitch, del. et lith.
Vincent Brooks, Imp.

Tab. 5075.

INGA macrophylla.

Large-leaved Inga.

Nat. Ord. Leguminosæ.—Polygamia Monœcia.

Gen. Char. Flores hermaphroditi vel rarius polygami. *Calyx* tubulosus vel campanulatus, 2–3-dentatus. *Corolla* tubulosa vel infundibuliformis. *Stamina* indefinita, sæpius numerosa, corolla duplo vel pluries longiora, basi in tubum coalita. *Ovarium* unicum. *Legumen* carnosum vel coriaceum, planum, tetragonum vel subteres, rectum vel subincurvum, vix dehiscens, marginibus incrassatis vel valde dilatatis et sulcatis. *Semina* pulpa dulci sæpe nivea involuta.—Frutices *vel* arbores *Americæ calidioris, inermes.* Folia *simpliciter abrupte pinnata;* petiolus *inter juga foliorum sæpe in alam expansus,* alis *semper ad nodos interruptis.* Glandulæ *inter omnia paria scutellatæ, turbinatæ, vel stipitatæ, in speciebus perpaucis obsoletæ vel plane nullæ.* Foliola *omnia opposita, paucijuga, majuscula (nunc maxima), —rarissime pollice minora,—sæpe pedalia, ex oblongo- vel lanceolato-ovata.* Flores *in umbellas, capitula, vel spicas oblongas vel rarius elongatas dispositi.* Spicæ *solitariæ vel sæpius fasciculatim pedunculatæ, axillares vel ad apices ramulorum foliis abortientibus paniculatæ.* Flores *sæpissime albi. Benth.*

Inga (§ Euinga) *macrophylla;* ramulis tetragonis ferrugineo-villoso-tomentosis, foliis junioribus parce hirtellis demum glabratis supra nitidis, petiolo rachique lato-alatis, foliolis 2–3-jugis subcoriaceo-membranaceis ovatis obovato-lanceolatisve brevi-acuminatis villosis demum glabratis supra nitidis subtus venis prominentibus basi obtusis vix subcordatis, stipulis lato-lanceolatis, pedunculo axillari solitario monocephalo petiolo longiore, capitulo globoso, floribus flavis sericeis, calyce tubuloso, corolla infundibuliformi calycem duplo excedente, staminibus longissimis.

Inga macrophylla. *H.B.K. Gen. et Sp. Am. v. 4. p.* 1015. *Benth. in Hook. Lond. Journ. Bot. v. 4. p.* 410. *Walp. Rep. Bot. v.* 5. *p.* 638.

Inga calocephala. *Pœpp. et Endl. Nov. Gen. et Sp. Pl. Peru. etc. v.* 3. *p.* 78 (*according to Bentham*).

Notwithstanding the able monograph of the genus *Inga* and of the *Mimoseæ* generally of Mr. Bentham in the Journal above quoted, I find the greatest difficulty in identifying the present species. The living plant was received from Linden in 1849, under the name of *Inga macrocephala,* to which plant, of H.B.K. at least, Mr. Bentham refers the *I. calocephala* of Pœppig and Endlicher; yet I find the characters given of the two somewhat

October 1st, 1858.

at variance, and that our plant agrees better with the latter than with the former. They are probably all three mere varieties of one species. Be that as it may, our species forms a handsome stove-shrub, which bore in April, 1857, for the first time, its beautiful heads of yellow flowers, quite silky from the numerous long filaments of the stamens.

Descr. Our plant of this forms a good-sized *shrub*, ten to twelve feet high. *Stems* terete, glabrous, much branched; the *branches* drooping, quadrangular, the younger ones clothed with dense, ferruginous, woolly hairs. *Leaves* consisting of two or three opposite pairs of *leaflets*, which are sessile, varying in length from four to eight or ten inches, coriaceo-membranaceous, glossy, slightly villous, ovate or obovate, shortly acuminate, closely penniveined, and the veins united by obliquely transversely parallel ones; paler beneath, where the veins are prominent. *Petiole* broadly winged, so as to have an obovate form; *rachis* too, between the two pairs, winged, giving a spathulate form, terminated between the superior pinnæ with a long spinule, and between the base of each pair of leaves is a large, scutellate, sessile *gland*. *Stipules* lanceolate, rather large. *Peduncle* solitary, axillary, villous, simple, twice the length of the petiole, bearing a globose sessile *head* of yellow flowers. *Calyx* cylindrical, two-lipped, downy. *Corolla* infundibuliform, five-cleft, villous. *Stamens* twice as long as the corolla, numerous. *Anthers* very small, abortive? *Ovary* oblong. *Style* as long as the stamens.

Fig. 1. Flower. 2. Pistil:—*magnified.*

W. [illegible] del. et lith.

Tab. 5076.

OUVIRANDRA Bernieriana.

Bernier's Lattice-leaf.

Nat. Ord. Juncagineæ.—Hexandria Monogynia.

Gen. Char. (*Vide supra*, Tab. 4894.)

Ouvirandra *Bernieriana;* foliis submersis anguste oblongo-ligulatis planis vel plerumque pertuso-fenestratis (parenchymate seriatim porosis poris quadratis), scapo superne inflato, spicis 3–5 fasciculatis gracilibus, floribus laxis roseis.

Ouvirandra Bernieriana. *Decaisne in Delessert Icones, v.* 3. *p.* 62. *t.* 100.

Gratifying as it was to us to publish a figure, from a living plant, of the rare *Ouvirandra fenestralis* from the lakes of Madagascar, it is no less so that we now publish a second species of the genus, collected during a subsequent visit to the same island, and by the same gentleman that introduced the former, the Rev. Henry Ellis. Messrs. Jackson and Son, of the Nursery, Kingston, have favoured us with the flowering plant here figured. We refer it with little hesitation to the *O. Bernieriana* of Professor Decaisne, notwithstanding he describes the leaves as made up wholly of parenchyme (not fenestrate). We have shown, in our account of the former species, that the leaves, especially while young, are not pertuse, the openings being closed with parenchyme: so in our present plant we have seen leaves which had the openings entirely filled up; but our most perfect state of the plant shows the parenchyme to be rather copious, so that the areoles formed by the longitudinal and transverse veins are perforated as it were with small square or four-angled *openings*, the largest next the costa, those next the margin almost obsolete. But this structure, so different from what is seen in the perfect foliage of *O. fenestralis*, is not the only difference, the leaves are longer and much narrower in proportion, almost ligulate, the reticulation smaller, the scape is inflated upwards; the spikes are four or five in number, fascicled, slender, and the flowers are lax and distant on the rachis, and pale rose-colour. Both kinds,

Mr. Ellis observes, in his letter to us, grow in the same waters, and he did not fail to note, on his last visit to Madagascar, that "one of the two had longer and narrower and less fenestrate leaves than the *O. fenestralis*," though, not seeing this in flower, he did not at once recognize it as distinct.

DESCR. *Leaves* all radical, tufted, submerged, from one and a half to two feet long, including the *petiole* (from four to six inches), oblong-ligulate, very slightly tapering at the base, obtuse at the point, formed of longitudinal and transverse fibres, which constitute a beautiful network on each side the costa; the *areoles* sometimes closed with parenchyme, more generally partially closed, leaving four-angled *openings* in the centre, of which the larger are next the midrib, and square, becoming smaller and forming transverse lines only near the margin. The colour is a brighter green than is exhibited by *Ouvirandra fenestralis*. *Petioles* subtriangular, channelled. *Peduncle*, or rather, *scape*, radical, swollen above the middle, and contracted again just below the inflorescence. *Spikes* three to five, forming a kind of umbel or fascicle of slender rachises, rather sparingly beset with flowers. *Bracts* two, sometimes three, oblong-spathulate, subtending each flower. *Perianth* proper, none. *Stamens* six; *filaments* stout, subulate. *Anthers* subglobose, two-celled. *Ovaries* three, apparently connected at the base, tapering into short, thick *styles*; *stigma* a depressed point.

Fig. 1. Portion of a leaf in its usual state. 2. Portion of a spike of flowers, with bracts. 3. Pistil:—*magnified.*

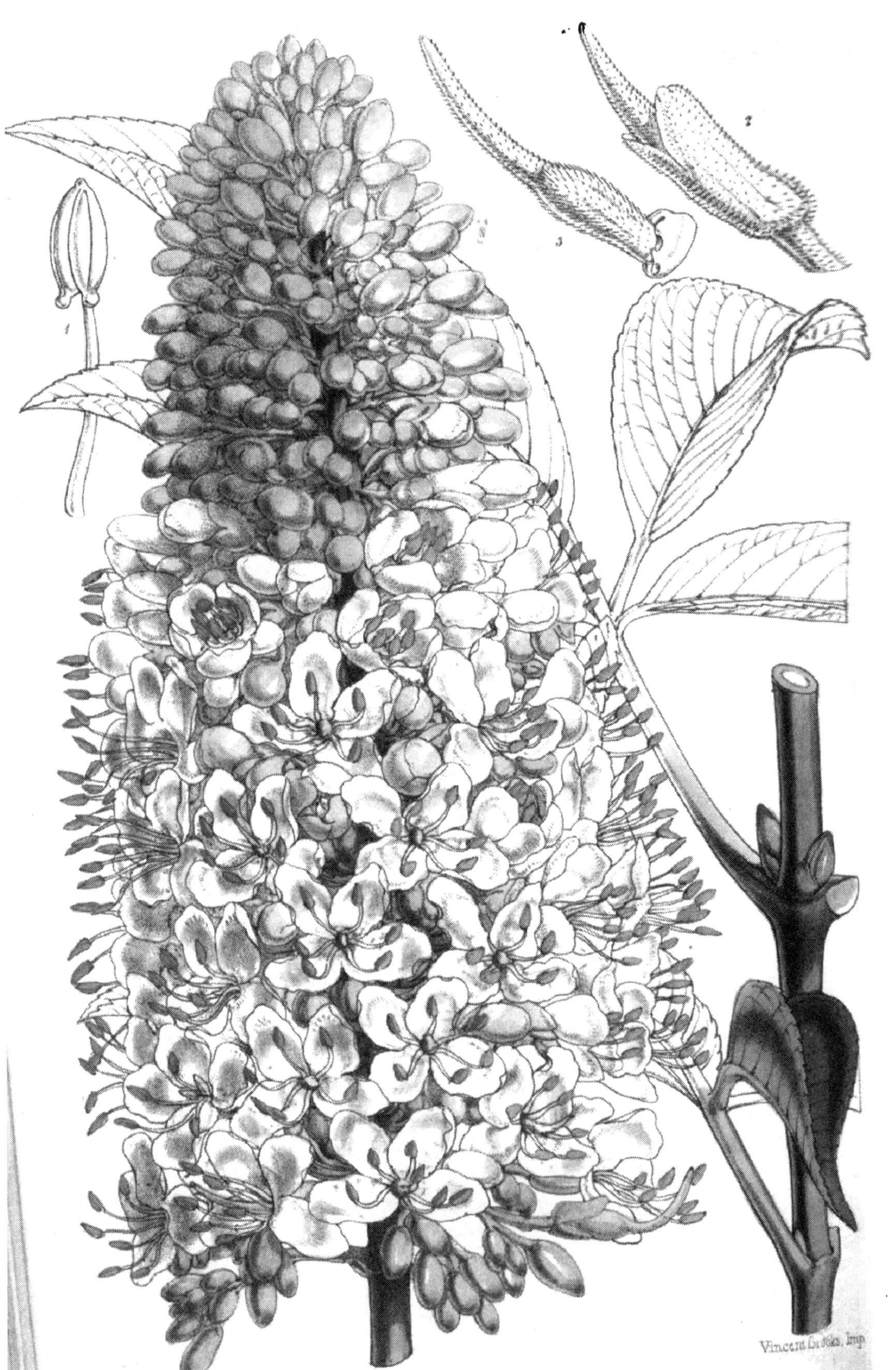
1
2
3
W. Fitch, del. et lith.
Vincent Brooks, Imp.

Tab. 5077.

ÆSCULUS Californica.

Cal fornian Buck-eye.

Nat. Ord. Hippocastaneæ.—Heptandria Monogynia.

Gen. Char. Flores polygami. *Cal.* campanulatus vel tubulosus, quinquefidus vel 5-dentatus, plus minus inæqualis. *Corollæ petala* 5, v. antici abortu 4, hypogyna, plus minus inæqualia et sæpe dissimilia, unguibus erectis, laminis patentibus. *Discus* annularis, integerrimus v. lobatus, sæpe unilateralis. *Stamina* 6–8, sæpissime 7, hypogyna, libera; *filamenta* filiformia, adscendentia; *antheræ* biloculares, longitudinaliter dehiscentes. *Ovarium* sessile, triloculare. *Ovula* in loculis gemina, angula centrali superposite inserta, inferius adscendens, superius appensum. *Stylus* filiformis; *stigma* acutum. *Capsula* coriacea, lævis v. echinata, trilocularis v. abortu bi-unilocularis, loculicide dehiscens, valvis medio septiferis. *Semina* in loculis abortu solitaria v. rarissime gemina; *testa* coriacea, nitida; *umbilico* basilari lato, deraso, exarillato. *Embryonis* exalbuminosi curvati *cotyledones* maximæ, carnosæ, conferruminatæ; *radicula* brevis, umbilico proxima; *plumula* diphylla.—Arbores *v.* frutices, *in India boreali et in America Boreali calidiore sponte crescentes;* foliis *oppositis, petiolatis, exstipulatis, palmatim quinque-novem-foliolatis;* foliolis *sessilibus vel petiolatis, penninerviis, serratis;* floribus *in racemos vel paniculas terminales thyrsoideas dispositis. Endl.*

Æsculus (§ Pavia) *Californica;* staminibus corolla longioribus, petalis 4, obovatis brevi-unguiculatis subæqualibus patentibus, calyce tubuloso bilabiato, thyrso multifloro compacto, foliolis 5 ovato-lanceolatis basi subangustatis rotundatis argute serratis glabris subtus pallidioribus.

Æsculus Californica. *Nutt. MS. Torr. et Gray, Fl. of N. Am. v.* 1. *p.* 251. *Nutt. Sylva, v.* 2. *p.* 69. *t.* 74. *Newberry in Williamson's Route to Calif. and Oregon,* 1855; *Bot. p.* 20. *f.* 1.

Calothyrsus Californica. *Spach in Ann. Sc. Nat. ser.* 2. *p.* 62.

The Californian Horse-Chestnut was probably first detected by Nuttall, at Monterey, and Drs. Torrey and Gray adopted his manuscript name. Seeds have been sent to Messrs. Veitch, from the Exeter and Chelsea Nurseries, and their young trees produced fine thyrsi of flowers in July, 1858. Mr. Newberry (from whom we have specimens by favour of Drs. Torrey and Gray) found it abundant in the Sacramento Valley; Mr. Bridges sends it to us from the same country. It is described as a low, spreading tree; the tallest seen by Mr. Newberry not more than twenty feet high. It has the merit of blossoming at an early age, and is remarkable for the dense clusters of flowers, said to be rose-coloured in the native country, but which are assuredly white in our specimen. It seems to be considered hardy in England. From the beauty of the flowers, and the long time during which they continue to appear, it would be a highly valuable acquisition to the cultivators of ornamental shrubs in the eastern States. The wood is soft, white, and brittle, like that of the other species of the genus.

DESCR. A small tree, with smaller leaves, if we may judge from our specimens, both cultivated and native, than those of our well-known *Æsculus Hippocastanum*, and of a firmer texture. *Leaflets* five, petiolulate, glabrous, ovato-lanceolate, moderately acuminate, closely penniveined. *Flowers* extremely numerous, in very dense terminal thyrsi, a span to a foot and more long. *Calyx* tubular, or between tubular and campanulate, green, tipped with red, at length two-lipped; *lips* unequal, erect or nearly so; upper one the largest, and three-toothed; lower one two-toothed. *Corolla* of four, nearly equal, obovate, slightly undulate, shortly clawed, spreading *petals*, white in our specimens; the two inferior ones are rather the largest, and more apart than the two superior ones. *Stamens* five to seven, longer than the petals. *Anthers* orange-coloured, ovate, bluntly apiculate, prolonged at the base of each cell into a blunt spur. *Ovary* oblong, attenuated at the base, where it is surrounded by an oblique, fleshy, crenated, glandular cup; at the apex tapering into a thick, subulate, villous *style*.

Fig. 1. Stamen. 2. Calyx and pistil. 3. Pistil and hypogynous gland:—*magnified.*

W. Fitch, del. et lith. Vincent Brooks, Imp.

TAB. 5078.

ŒNOTHERA BISTORTA; var. *Veitchiana*.

Twisted-fruited Œnothera; Mr. Veitch's var.

Nat. Ord. ONAGRARIEÆ.—OCTANDRIA MONOGYNIA.

Gen. Char. (*Vide supra*, TAB. 3764.)

ŒNOTHERA (§ Sphærostigma) *bistorta*; pubescens ramosa viridis, caulibus herbaceis erecto-decumbentibus, foliis ovato-lanceolatis acute dentatis inferioribus petiolatis supremis ovato-acuminatis sessilibus, floribus in racemum foliosum (tunc axillaribus) v. bracteatum terminalem dispositis, tubo calycis infundibuliformis lobis breviore, petalis obovato-rotundatis staminibus duplo longioribus, stigmate magno globoso velutino, capsulis quadrangularibus demum insigniter tortis.

ŒNOTHERA bistorta. *Nutt. MS. Torrey and Gray, Fl. of N. America, v.* 1. *p.* 508.

ŒNOTHERA heterophylla. *Nutt. MS., not of Spach* (*Torrey and Gray*).

HOLOSTIGMA Bottæ. *Spach, Onagr. p.* 16?

Var. *Veitchii*, floribus majoribus speciosis. (TAB. NOSTR. 5078.)

We have here an *Œnothera* of South California, imported by Messrs. Veitch, of the Exeter and Chelsea Nurseries, from San Gabriel, through Mr. William Lobb. That it is the *Œnothera bistorta* of Nuttall, of which we have authentic specimens in our herbarium, there can be, we think, no doubt; but it is equally certain that, like other species of the genus, it is liable to vary much in form and clothing of the foliage, and in the size and beauty of the flowers. Our native specimen, from Mr. Lobb (n. 416), of this very plant gives no idea of the plant in cultivation, which, we think, promises to be one of the best of any yellow-flowered plants for bedding out, the stems being of humble stature, the flowers large and copious with a copious succession on the racemes, and when fully expanded, the petals exhibit a dark-orange or blood-coloured spot at the base of each petal, as in some of the *Cistus* tribe. Messrs. Torrey and Gray have already noticed one variety with the capsules

OCTOBER 1ST, 1858.

completely coiled when mature; but on the same specimen we often find every form of coiling, reminding one very much of the appearance of a worm in various degrees of contortion. The species seems peculiar to South California; Nuttall found it at San Diego; yet the plant is perfectly suited to our summer climate, where it ripens its seeds, or may be increased by cuttings. The curious stigma is characteristic of the section *Sphærostigma*.

Descr. Annual, pubescent, but not hoary. *Stems* simple or branched, subdecumbent, terete, green, tinged with red on one side. *Leaves* rather distant, lower ones shortly petiolate, lanceolate, acuminate; upper ones broader and sessile, gradually passing into bracts, all of them dentate, the upper ones more deeply so, penniveined. *Flowers* solitary in the axil of almost every leaf and bract, short-pedicellate (but the slender ovary has very much the appearance of a peduncle). *Calyx;* its long narrow four-angled *tube* adherent with the ovary, except the apex, which is infundibuliform and free. *Segments* four, lanceolate, reflexed. *Petals* broadly cuneato-rotundate, spreading, full yellow, with small, deep blood-coloured spots at the base. *Stamens* eight, alternately shorter, and the tallest much shorter than the petals. *Style* as long as the stamens. *Stigma* very large, velvety, capitate, yellow. *Fruit* linear, four-angled, one and a half to two inches long, four-angled, singularly contorted, and even twisted, as it advances to maturity.

Fig. 1. Upper portion of the ovary, with calyx, segments, and stamens. 2. Single petal:—*magnified.*

5079.
1
2
3
4
5
6
Vincent Brooks, Imp.

Tab. 5079.

TRADESCANTIA discolor; var. *variegata*.

Purple-leaved Spiderwort; variegated var.

Nat. Ord. Commelyneæ.—Hexandria Monogynia.

Gen. Char. Flores regulares. *Sepala* 6, libera, patentia; tria exteriora navicularia, persistentia; tria interiora majora, petaloidea, breviter unguiculata, marcescendo-persistentia. *Stamina* 6, subhypogyna, omnia fertilia. *Filamenta* libera, plerumque barbata. *Antheræ* conformes, loculis reniformibus, connexivo varia forma distinctis, interdum tres sepalis exterioribus oppositæ robustiores, loculis replicatis extrorsæ filamentisque brevioribus sustentæ. *Ovarium* sessile, triloculare; *ovula* in loculis 2, superposita. *Stylus* 1. *Stigma* simplex, obtusum, infundibulare vel peltato-ampliatum. *Capsula* trilocularis, trivalvis; valvis medio septiferis. *Semina* bina, superposita, angulata.—Herbæ *Americanæ, erectæ vel diffusæ, sæpe repentes.* Folia *indivisa.* Vaginæ *integræ.* Pedunculi *axillares et terminales, solitarii, gemini v. plures, apice umbellato-pauci-multiflori, sæpe brevissimi, subnulli, folioque duplici involucrati. Kth.*

Tradescantia *discolor;* aloidea, caule brevi erecto, foliis lanceolatis acuminatis subtus violaceis, pedunculis axillaribus, bracteis insigniter equitantibus compressis flores omnino involucrantibus.

Tradescantia discolor. *L'Hérit. Sert. Angl. v.* 8. *t.* 12. *Ait. Hort. Kew. v.* 5. *p.* 403. *Smith, Ic. Pict. t.* 10. *Willd. Sp. Pl. v.* 2. *p.* 18. *Ker in Bot. Mag. t.* 1192. *Red. Liliac. t.* 168. *Kth. Enum. Pl. v.* 4. *p.* 85.

Tradescantia spathacea. *Sw. Fl. Ind. Occ. v.* 1. *p.* 607.

Var. *variegata;* foliis supra flavo-vittatis. (Tab. Nostr. 5079.)

Tradescantia variegata, *Hort.*

We cannot say much in praise of the figure of the ordinary state of this very peculiar plant, published at Tab. 1192 of this work, by Mr. Ker, and we are glad of an opportunity to do more justice to it, in representing a state of the plant that has lately been cultivated in gardens, imported, we believe, from Belgium, under the name of *Trad. variegata.* It is remarkable for the rich colour of the under side of the leaves, and the variegated yellowish lines on the dark-green upper side. The species inhabits Mexico, where it is considered to be an aboriginal, but it is cultivated in various of the islands in the Gulf of Mexico, and in the East as well as the West Indies. It is easily increased by cuttings, and this state of the plant especially is worthy of cultivating in every stove or warm greenhouse. It flowers during the summer months.

Descr. Var. *variegata.* The *rhizome,* rather than stem, is short and ascending. The *leaves* are numerous from the summit of the rhizome, somewhat aloid, lanceolate, firm, rather thick and fleshy, sheathing at the base, dark-green above, with pale-yellow streaks running longitudinally, as in the well-known "Ribbon-grass," but the lines are less distinct, the back of the leaves has a blunt keel, and the colour is a rich purple. *Peduncles* short, thick, axillary, not rising above the sheathing base of the leaf, bearing three large *bracteæ,* which are complicate, compressed, the two upper ones opposite to each other, and completely equitant, so as to form a compressed cup or *involucre,* resembling a bivalve-shell (some large *Tellina*), of a purple colour, within which the *flowers* appear, and which are but slightly, if at all, protruded: these flowers are pure white. *Calyx* of three, ovate, spreading sepals. *Corolla* of three, nearly cordate, spreading petals, larger than the calyx. *Stamens* six. *Filaments* filiform, singular, tortuose, bearing a tuft of long, jointed hairs below the middle. *Anthers* all perfect, transversely oblong, subdidymous, yellow. *Ovary* globose. *Style* subulate. *Capsule* small, subbaccate, three-celled, red.

Fig. 1. Flower-bud. 2. Flower expanded. 3. Stamen. 4. Pistil:—*magnified.* 5. Capsule, *nat. size.* 6. Transverse section of ditto, *magnified.*

5080.

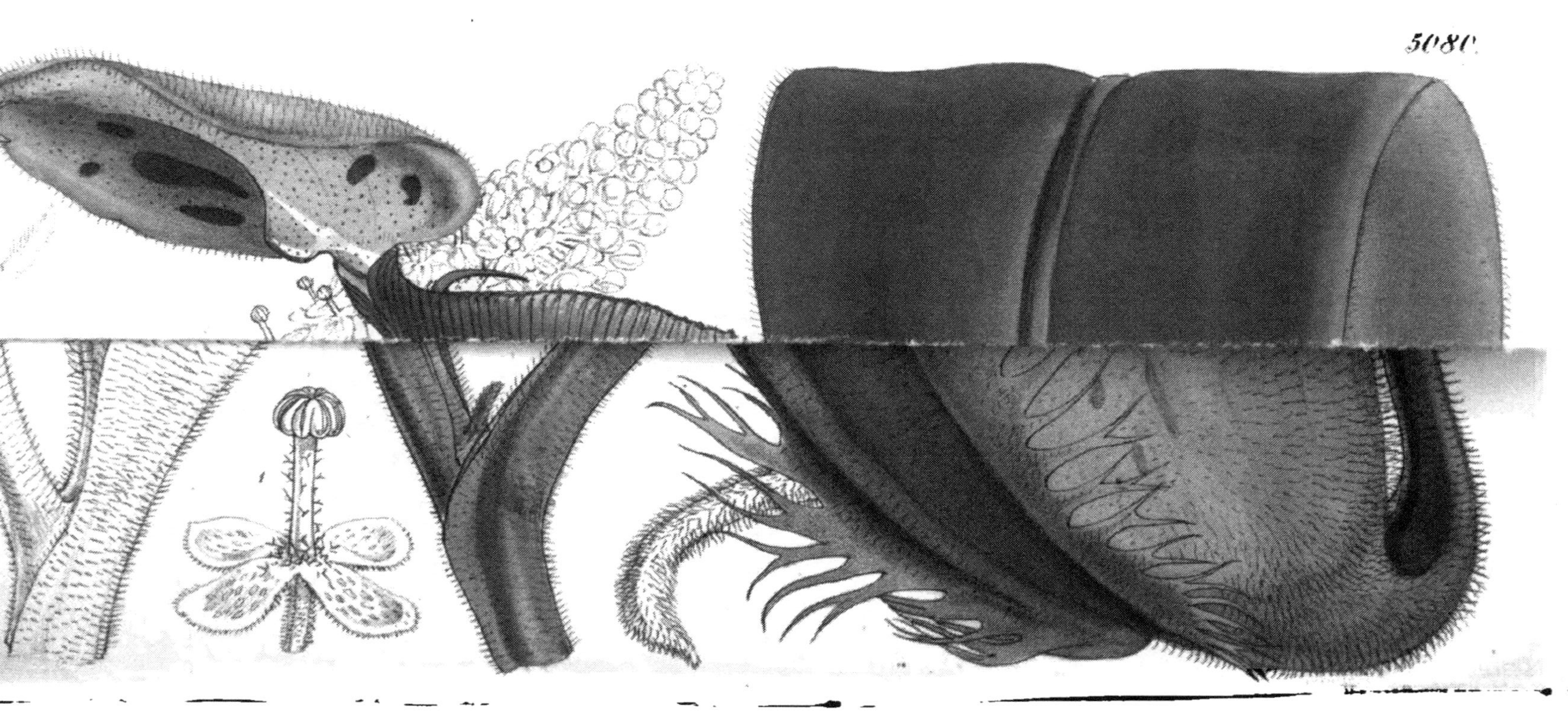

TAB. 5080.

NEPENTHES VILLOSA.

Villous Pitcher-plant.

Nat. Ord. NEPENTHACEÆ.—DIŒCIA MONODELPHIA.

Gen. Char. (*Vide supra*, TAB. 4285.)

NEPENTHES *villosa;* rufescenti-villosa, foliis petiolatis, ascidiis caulinis amplissimis cylindraceis antice lamellis duabus longitudinalibus longe fimbriatis, oris insigniter elongati valde obliqui margine latissimo reflexo plicatim striato, operculo ovato demum erecto facie interiore punctata punctis copiosis excavatis versus apicem majoribus basi medio carinato.

NEPENTHES villosa. *Hook. fil. in Icones Plant. Rar. v.* 9. *t.* 888.

Dried flowering specimens only, and unfortunately without the perfect ascidia or pitchers, of what we believe to be the same plant as that here figured, were sent by Hugh Low, Jun., Esq., gathered on Kina-Baloo, in Borneo, growing at an elevation of about 8000 feet above the level of the sea. Mr. Thomas Lobb was more fortunate in sending to Messrs. Veitch and Sons, Exeter and Chelsea Nursery, living plants from mountains near Sarawak, together with dried flowering specimens, from which our accompanying figures are taken. It as much excels *N. Rafflesiana* in the peculiarity of the ascidia, as that does all previously known species. They are more than a foot long, and the curious broad margins to the sides of the elongated mouth resemble the gills of a fish in structure and size, and almost in colour.

DESCR. The figure of this curious plant will give a better idea of its general structure than any words can do. The plant is, like it congeners, a climber, very hairy, and even extremely villous in its young state, but in age the copious spreading hairs, in our specimens at least, are evidently more or less deciduous. *Leaves* alternate, on rather long, sheathing *petioles*, expanding into the oval or more or less oblong and elongated *blade*, from six inches to a foot long, spreading, and generally decurved, subcoriaceo-membranaceous, entire, furnished with a strong central *costa*, nerveless; this costa is continued for four to six inches, more or less, beyond the blade or lamina, and produces a young pitcher (*ascidium*) at its extremity. The weight, it would appear,

NOVEMBER 1ST, 1858.

of this pitcher, causes the prolonged costa and the upper half of the blade of the leaf to descend, taking a downward direction; nevertheless, as the pitcher enlarges this has always an upward tendency, and becomes quite erect, from a span to a foot long; in an early stage closed by the lid, at which time the curious fringe at the mouth, while covered with the lid, is very small, as would appear from our young dried specimens; but as our living specimen possesses only a perfectly formed pitcher, we shall confine our present description to that. Its general form is cylindrical, nine inches in circumference, somewhat ventricose or unequal-sided, rather suddenly tapering below into the prolonged costa: it is furnished in front for its whole length with two longitudinal membranaceous wings, cut into long, simple, or bi- or tri-fid segments; the uppermost segments the longest and the most divided. The *substance* of this pitcher is membranaceous, but firm, the *colour* a pale fulvous-green, blotched with purplish-brown, and the wings are of that colour: the surface is obscurely reticulately veined, and is more or less hairy. The mouth or opening is the most extraordinary portion of this pitcher; it is very oblique, its margin formed of a substance distinct in texture and colour from the rest of the pitcher, of considerable breadth (two inches in the widest portion), of a fleshy nature, recurved, orange-purple, beautifully plaited or radiated with elevated lamellated lines, extending *upwards* to its narrowest portion, where the lips of the margin meet, project in a keel-like form, closing over that part of the mouth. The apex is terminated by the *lid*. This, in its perfect state, stands nearly erect, is ovato-cordate, apiculate, downy, with a keel or crest at the base beneath: its whole under side is impresso-punctate, with dots which are quite visible to the naked eye. The *colour* is green, margined and spotted with blood-colour. The lower part of the mouth is thus alone pervious, and that very much contracted. In the inside of the pitchers water is naturally collected, and, as in other species of the genus, no doubt, is a great provision of nature for decoying and for the destruction of insects. The petioles of the leaves are deeply channelled above. Our dried flowering specimen affords a lateral pedunculated raceme of downy *male flowers*. *Perianth* of four spreading obovate *sepals*. *Column* of stamens bearing a few branched hairs. *Anthers* six, arranged in a capitate whorl.

Our Plate represents the young portion of a male plant with flowers (from our native dried specimens), and a portion of Messrs. Veitch's cultivated plant, with a fully formed pitcher, *natural size*. 2. Single male flower, *magnified*.

5081.

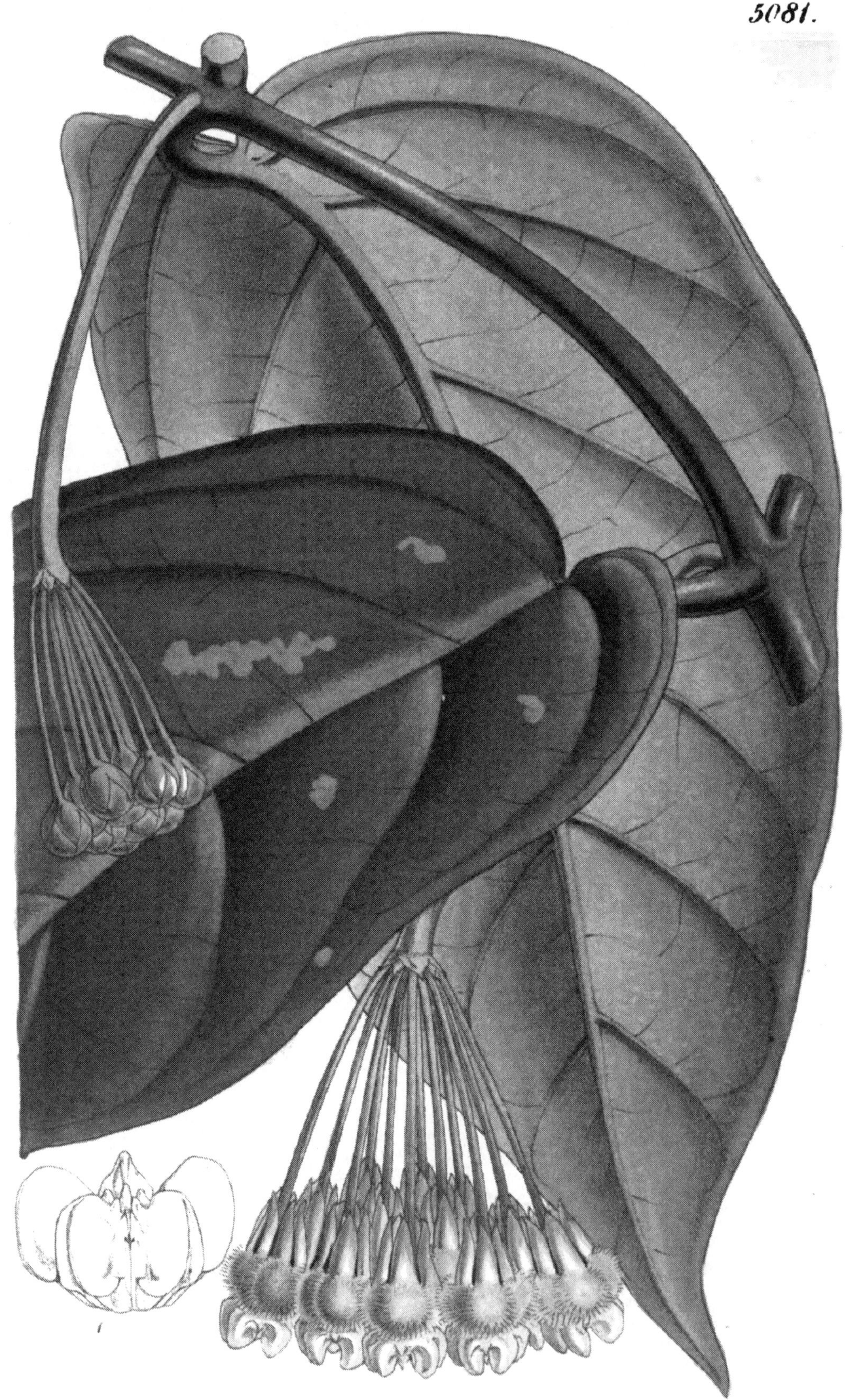

W Fitch del et lith

Tab. 5081.

PLOCOSTEMMA lasianthum.

Woolly-flowered Plocostemma.

Nat. Ord. Asclepiadeæ.—Pentandria Digynia.

Gen. Char. Plocostemma, *Bl. Calyx* quinquepartitus. *Corolla* quinquefida, patens v. reflexa, intus ad basin stuposa. *Corona staminea* pentaphylla, gynostegio subsessili adnata; *foliolis* carnosis, erectis, compressis, subtus conduplicatis, angulo interiore in dentem antheræ incumbentem producto. *Antheræ* membrana stigmati incumbente terminatæ. *Pollinia* basi affixa, erecta, oblonga, compressa, hinc marginata. *Stigma* apiculatum. *Folliculi* . . .—Frutices *Archipelagi Indici, volubiles;* foliis *oppositis, coriaceis, subvenosis, glabris;* umbellis *pedunculatis, terminalibus v. interpetiolaribus, multifloris. Bl.*

Plocostemma *lasianthum;* foliis ovalibus breviter cuspidato-acuminatis venosis, umbellis longe pedunculatis pendentibus, corolla reflexa intus ad basin dense stuposa.

Plocostemma lasianthum. *Blume in Rumphia, v.* 4. *p.* 30; *Mus. Bot. Lugd.-Bat. v.* 1. *p.* 60. *f.* 14.

Hoya lasiantha. *Herb. Korthals. (Blume).*

We are favoured with this remarkable Asclepiadeous plant by Mr. Low, of the Clapton Nursery, who imported it from Borneo. It proves to be a genus of the family allied to *Hoya* which Professor Blume has lately established in his 'Rumphia,' and figured in his valuable 'Museum Botanicum Lugduno-Batavorum,' differing from *Hoya*, but having the foliola of the staminal crown erect, compressed, conduplicate beneath, and the corolla at the base within densely woolly. The author characterizes two species, both natives of the Malay Islands; the present one peculiar, as far as yet known, to Borneo. It flowers with us in July.

Descr. A long-stemmed, climbing *shrub*, with quite the habit of a *Hoya;* the *branches* terete, dark-green, glabrous, as in every part of the plant, save the corolla. *Leaves* opposite, petiolate, a span long, oval, or rather ovate, subcordate at the base, apiculato-acuminate, thick, fleshy, dark-green, especially above, with occasionally a few pale blotches, veined; principal *veins* very distinct in the recent leaf. *Petiole* about an inch long, terete. *Peduncle* interpetiolary in our specimen, long, pendent, thickened and dilated at the apex, where it bears an *umbel* or rather a *fascicle* of a considerable number of *flowers*, all hanging downwards, of a tawny-orange colour. *Calyx* small, five-lobed. *Corolla* rotate, of five ovate segments, which segments are strongly reflexed upon the pedicel, and the margins are recurved; the disc of the corolla cushioned, as it were, with a dense cottony mass, mixed with patent hairs. *Staminal crown* singularly large and as described above.

Fig. 1. Staminal crown, *magnified*.

5082.
1
2
3
W Fitch, del. et lith.
Vincent Brooks, Imp.

Tab. 5082.

THUNBERGIA NATALENSIS.

Natal Thunbergia.

Nat. Ord. Acanthaceæ.—Didynamia Angiospermia.

Gen. Char. (*Vide supra*, Tab. 4119.)

Thunbergia *Natalensis;* erecta basi frutescens glabriuscula, foliis subapproximatis ovatis acutis sessilibus 3–5-nerviis margine sinuato-dentato, pedunculis axillaribus solitariis unifloris folio subbrevioribus, bracteis ovatis subacuminatis 3-nerviis reticulatis, corollæ tubo flavo bracteas superante, limbo cæruleo, calycis dentibus 5 latis triangularibus obtusis incurvis, antheris bicornibus, stylo superne dilatato glanduloso in stigmate concavo triangulari expanso.

Native of Natal, whence the Messrs. Veitch, of the Exeter and Chelsea Nurseries, received seeds through Mr. Cuming, and reared plants which flowered in the greenhouse in July, 1858. Its nearest affinity is doubtless with *Thunbergia atriplicifolia* of E. Meyer; like that, having sessile and angulately-toothed leaves: but these leaves in our plant are almost quite glabrous and much larger and broader; and there is a peculiar character in the five broad teeth or segments of the calyx, and very different from the numerous spine-like segments of that of *R. atriplicifolia*,—a native however of the same country, where it appears to be extremely plentiful, for we have received specimens from various correspondents,—whereas our only acquaintance with the present species is through Messrs. Veitch's cultivated specimens. Probably Mr. Bentham's *Meyenia erecta*, from tropical W. Africa, figured at our Tab. 5013, may be safely referred to *Thunbergia*. It has not a few points in common with the present plant, but the anthers (supposing them to be correct as represented by our artist) and the calyx are very different, as well as the stigma: and the corolla is very inferior in point of colour.

Descr. *Stem* erect, two feet or more high, somewhat shrubby below, above herbaceous, green, quadrangular, glabrous except at the internodes. *Leaves* opposite, the pairs rather approximate, sessile, ovate, acute or subacuminate, sinuato-serrate, with three primary *veins*, glabrous above, hairy on the costa and veins beneath. *Peduncles* axillary, solitary, erect, single-flowered, much shorter than the leaves. *Flowers* horizontally drooping, large, handsome. *Bracts* ovate, nearly as long as the tube of the corolla, to which they are appressed, three-nerved; *nerves* strong, reticulated with lesser veins. *Corolla* with the *tube* yellow, two inches long, curved upwards; *limb* large, cut into five broad, obcordate, nearly equal, horizontally spreading *lobes*. *Calyx* minute, of six, small, triangular, incurved, apiculate teeth. *Stamens* four, nearly equal in height. *Anthers* each two-horned. *Ovary* surrounded by a large, fleshy *disc*. *Style* slender at the base, glabrous, gradually enlarged into a somewhat trumpet-shaped but triangular concave *stigma*, with numerous glandular *hairs* below the stigma.

Fig. 1. Stamens. 2. Calyx and pistil. 3. Stigma:—*magnified*.

5083.

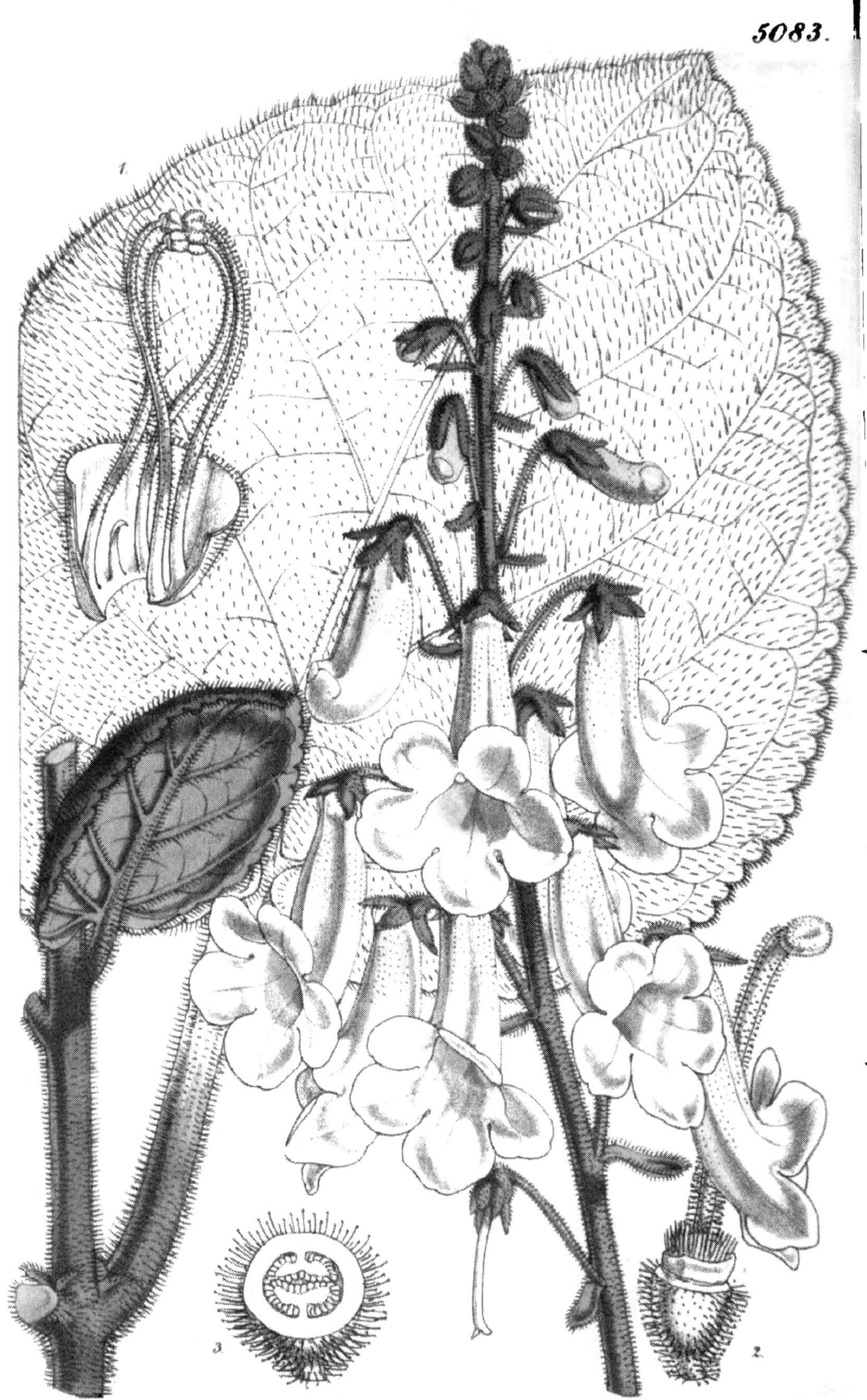

W. Fitch, del. et lith. Vincent Brooks, Imp.

Tab. 5083.

NÆGELIA multiflora.

White-flowered Nægelia.

Nat. Ord. Gesneraceæ.—Didynamia Gymnospermia.

Gen. Char. Corolla oblique adnata, *tubo* ventre inflato, *limbo* inæqualiter quinquelobo, *fauce* late hiante. *Annulus* perigynus quinquecrenatus. *Stigma* capitatum. Reliqua ut *Gesneriæ.*—Herbæ *stolonibus perennantes;* foliis *oppositis;* floribus *racemosis, ante anthesin revolutis. Regel.*

Nægelia *multiflora;* caulescens molliter pubescens glanduloso-villosa, foliis (amplis) longe petiolatis cordatis crenatis, racemis elongatis multifloris, corollæ (albæ) tubo elongato superne angulato apice sursum curvato vix ventricoso limbi valde obliqui lobis patentibus subæqualibus, stylo glanduloso-piloso.

Gloxinia? multiflora. *Martens et Gal. En. Pl. Mex. Gesnera, p.* 3. *Herb. Gal. n.* 1913.

Nægelia amabilis. *Hort.*

Achimenes (Nægelia) amabilis. *Dcne. in Fl. des Serres, for* 1857, *p.* 1192.

This plant is so closely allied to the well-known *Gesnera zebrina* (see our Tab. 3940), that at first sight I was disposed to consider it a white-flowered state of that beautiful species. The nature of the clothing, however, is different; the form of the flower (as well as the colour) is different, and approximates to that of our *Gloxinia tubiflora* (Tab. 3971). Dr. Regel, who has studied with great attention the whole Gesneraceous family, and given excellent figures of his genera, separates *Gesnera zebrina* from the true *Gesneræ*, under the name of *Nægelia.* Whether or not the distinguishing marks are of sufficient importance to constitute a valid genus, the present individual must rank with it. Living plants have been received, from the Belgian Gardens, at Kew, under the name of *Nægelia amabilis,* but it appears identical with Martens and Galeotti's *Gloxinia? multiflora,* a native of the eastern Cordillera of Oaxaca, at an elevation of 2–3000 feet above the level of the sea. It flowers with us in the stove in the autumnal months.

Descr. The general aspect of the plant, the shape and size of the foliage, etc., bear a great resemblance to *Nægelia* (Gesnera) *zebrina;* but here, besides the soft velvety clothing, there are copious patent hairs generally tipped with a gland. *Raceme* terminal, elongated. *Pedicels* bracteolated at the base, erecto-patent. *Flowers* drooping, shorter than the pedicels, white or cream-colour. *Calyx* almost hispid with glandular hairs. *Corolla* with the *tube* scarcely ventricose, elongated, curved upwards, below the very oblique, rather large, spreading, five-lobed, equal *limb*. *Glandular ring* nearly entire, crowning the ovary; from within, and from the apex of the ovary, arises a circle of bristles. *Style* glanduloso-pilose. *Stigma* capitate, umbilicate.

Fig. 1. Stamen. 2. Pistil. 3. Transverse section of the ovary:—*magnified*.

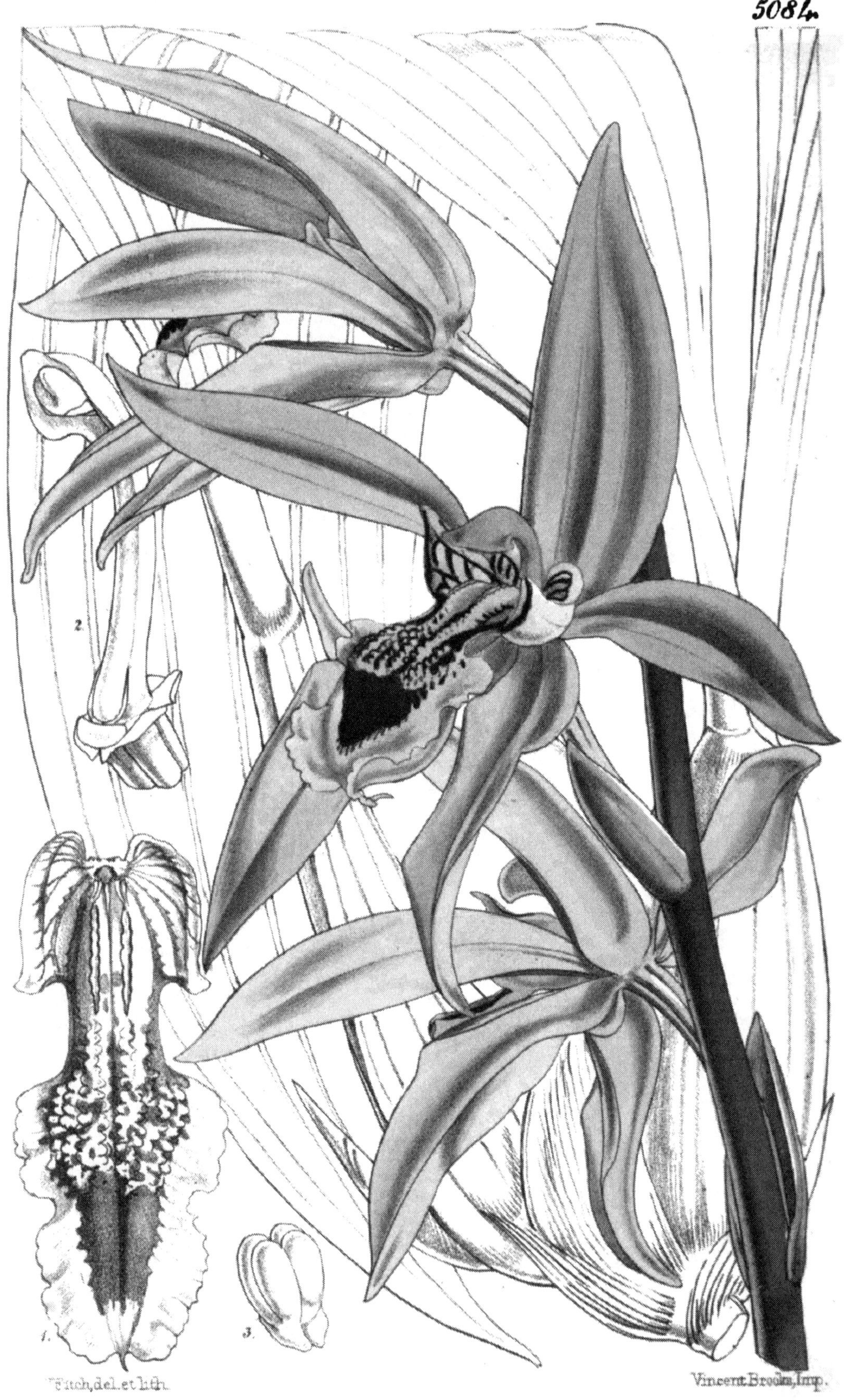
5084.
2.
1.
3.
Fitch, del. et lith.
Vincent Brooks, Imp.

Tab. 5084.

CŒLOGYNE PANDURATA.

Pandurate Cœlogyne.

Nat. Ord. Orchideæ.—Gynandria Monandria.

Gen. Char. (*Vide supra*, Tab. 5001.)

Cœlogyne (§ Flaccidæ)* *pandurata;* foliis maximis multinerviis, racemo longo pendulo, bracteis oblongis cucullatis distantibus persistentibus, petalis sepalisque lineari-oblongis, labello basi concavo cordato-oblongo retuso cis apicem crispo setaceo-acuminato (lateribus deflexis pandurato), lobis basilaribus nanis acuminatis, disco lævi tricarinato utrinque crista alta duplici verruculosa aucto citra cristam copiose verrucoso.

Cœlogyne pandurata. *Lindley in Gard. Chron. Dec.* 10, 1853; *Folia Orchidacea, part* 5, *Cœlogyne, p.* 3.

This very fine Orchideous plant is so very unlike the hitherto best-known species of *Cœlogyne* (generally showy and highly ornamental, white or rose-colour, more or less mottled with yellow and dark-purple), that at first sight it would not be easily recognized as belonging to the genus: yet it possesses all the characters. Indeed it is rare for flowers of any genus to be so truly green as in the present plant. It is a native of Borneo, imported by Mr. Low, of the Clapton Nursery, and described by Dr. Lindley in the works above quoted, from a flowering plant in the possession of Messrs. Loddiges, Hackney Nursery, December, 1853. Although a native specimen from Mr. Low, Jun., is in the Hookerian Herbarium, sent to us by Mr. Low, Jun., from Borneo, we have not ourselves had the advantage of seeing the living plant. The accompanying figure is from a fine specimen in the Orchideous House of — Butler, Esq., Park Place, Woolwich. We therefore take advantage of Dr. Lindley's description in most of what follows.

Descr. *Pseudobulbs* oblong-ovate, rather large, slightly compressed. *Leaves* very large, broad-lanceolate, longitudinally striated and plaited. *Raceme* about as long as the leaves (eighteen

* This section (*Flaccidæ*) is known by its long pendulous racemes.

November 1st, 1858.

or twenty inches). "*Flowers* about two inches apart, green, in a pendent *raceme*, furnished with brown (green when young), cucullate, deciduous *bracts*, as long as the peduncle. Each *flower* is about four inches across if fully expanded, with pale-green *sepals* and *petals*, and a singularly warted *lip*, marked with deep broad black veins and stains upon a greenish-yellow ground. The *crests* are two, deep, double-warted lines, on each side of a three-ribbed, central *disc;* these crests converge towards the middle of the *lip*, where they lose themselves in a field of pallid, rugged, irregularly situated, often two-lobed warts. The *column* is green, slightly expanded into thin, rounded edges. The *lip*, although really oblong, yet, in consequence of the manner in which the sides are bent down, has much the form of a violin. A memorandum (of Mr. Low, Jun.) in the Hookerian Herbarium states the flower to emit an agreeable perfume."—*Lindley.*

Fig. 1. The lip, *nat. size.* 2. The column. 3. Pollen-masses :—*magnified.*

W Fitch, del.et lith.

Vincent Brooks. Imp.

TAB. 5085.

OSBECKIA ASPERA.

Rough-leaved Osbeckia.

Nat. Ord. MELASTOMACEÆ.—OCTANDRIA MONOGYNIA.

Gen. Char. *Calycis tubus* ovatus, sæpius setis stellatis aut pube stellata vestitus; *lobi* 4–5, persistentes aut decidui; *appendices* inter lobos extus ortæ, forma et magnitudine variæ. *Petala* 4–5; *stamina* 8–10, filamentis glabris, antheris subæqualibus brevi-rostratis, connectivo basi breve biauriculato. *Ovarium* apice setosum. *Capsula* 4–5-locularis. *Semina* cochleata.—Herbæ *aut sæpius* suffrutices *Americanæ, Africanæ, et Asiaticæ.* Folia *integerrima,* 3–5-*nervia.* Flores *terminali. DC.*

OSBECKIA *aspera;* fruticosa, rami junioribus subquadrangularibus strigosis, foliis petiolatis ovalibus acutis 3–5-nerviis superne strigosis subtus rigide pubescentibus ad nervos hispidis, racemis terminalibus paucifloris, calycis tubo hemisphærico setoso superne squamuloso, squamulis longe rigide stellatim setosis, staminibus 10, antheris uniformibus apice rostratis basi bituberculatis, ovario longe setoso.

OSBECKIA aspera. *Wight et Arn. Prodr. Fl. Penins. Ind. Or. p.* 323. *Wight, Ic. Plant. Ind. Or. n.* 377. *t.* 377. *Walp. Repert. v.* 2. *p.* 581. *Naudin, Melast. p.* 74.

MELASTOMA asperum. *Linn. Sp. Pl. p.* 560. *De Cand. Prodr. v.* 3. *p* 145.

ASTEROSTOMA asperum. *Blume, Mus. Bot. Lugd.-Batav. v.* 1. *p.* 50.

This has been for many years cultivated in the stoves of the Royal Gardens of Kew, where, during the summer and autumnal months, it makes a very handsome appearance, with its strongly three-nerved leaves and its copious, large, rich purple-coloured blossoms. It is a native of Ceylon and the peninsula of India, and is well figured in Dr. Wight's 'Icones Plantarum Indiæ Orientalis.' We are disposed to think that Wight and Arnott were correct in referring hither the *Osbeckia glauca,* Benth. in Wall. Cat. n. 4073 (and in our herbarium), from Travancore and Trincomalee,—a plant, too, of Dr. Wight's own gathering, but that the accurate Naudin pronounces the two distinct, and describes them as such accordingly; at least, he does so with "*Osbeckia glauca*" of Wall. MSS., meaning probably thereby of his Cata-

DECEMBER 1ST, 1858.

logue. References for this plant to Rheed. Hort. Malab. v. 4. t. 43, and Rumph. Amboyn. v. 4. t. 71, are justly considered doubtful.

Descr. A small *shrub*, one to two feet and more high; the young *branches* subquadrangular, strigose. *Leaves* opposite, oval or approaching to ovate, acute, petiolate (*petiole* scarcely half an inch long, generally red), strongly three- to five-nerved, firm, subcoriaceous, entire; above, strigose with close-pressed rigid short hairs or bristles; beneath, coarsely downy and hispid upon the prominent nerves. *Flowers* subracemose and terminating short *branches*, only one on each branch opening at a time: these are very handsome. The *calyx-tube* is between hemispherical and bell-shaped, clothed with coarse bristles; towards the upper part and on the outside of the calyx-lobes are small scales, terminated by long stellate bristles; *limb* of five lobes, spreading, deciduous. *Petals* five, large, obcordate, rich purple, spreading horizontally, slightly waved. *Stamens* ten; *filaments* moderately long, and nearly equal; *anthers* uniform, linear, slightly spirally twisted, beaked at the apex and opening by a pore, and at the base having a small *annulus*, with a small two-lobed process in front. *Ovary* crowned at the summit with copious long bristles, which project beyond the mouth of the calyx; *style* bent down in a direction opposite to that of the stamens; *stigma* obtuse.

Fig. 1. Calyx and pistil. 2. Stamen:—*magnified.*

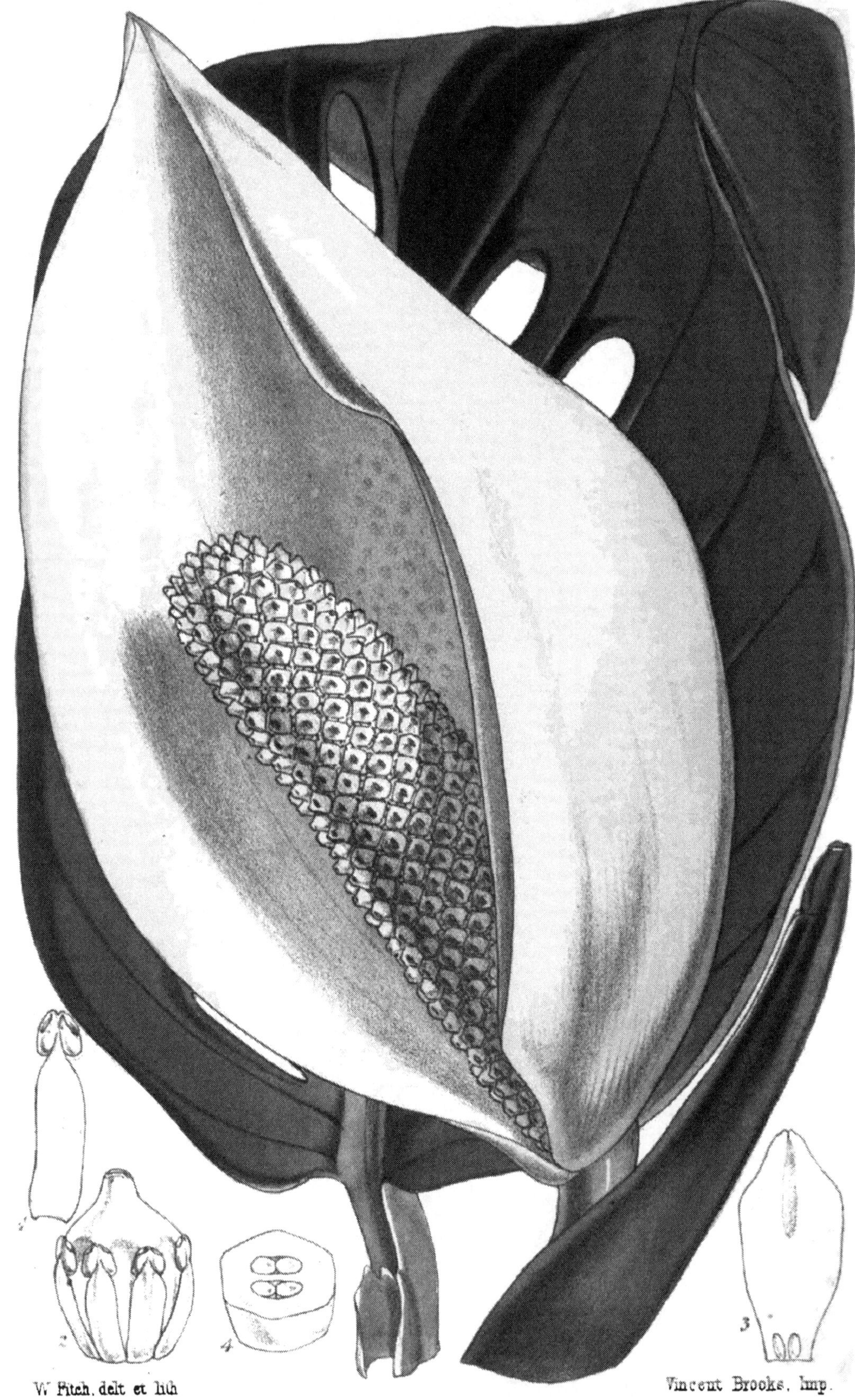

W. Fitch, delt et lith

Vincent Brooks, Imp.

Tab. 5086.

MONSTERA Adansonii.

Perforated Monstera.

Nat. Ord. Aroideæ: Trib. Callaceæ.—Heptandria Monogynia.

Gen. Char. Spatha hians, tandem decidua. *Spadix* sessilis, basi fœmineus. *Ovaria* bilocularia, loculis biovulatis, *ovulis* infimæ axeos parti affixis erectis. *Stylus* brevis, manifestus. *Stigma* capitatum. *Fructus: baccæ* connatæ, epicarpia tandem abjicientes.—Americæ tropicæ *incolæ*, caule *scandente*, foliis *ovato-oblongis integris v. perforatis*, petiolis *vagina latiuscula dilatatis*, spatha *ex albido flava*, ovariis *raphidophoris*. *Schott.*

Monstera *Adansonii;* scandens, foliis oblongo-ovatis cordatis pertusis, spathis cymbiformibus.

Monstera Adansonii. *Schott, Meletem. Bot. p.* 21. *Kunth, Enum. Plant. v.* 3. *p.* 60.

Dracontium pertusum. *Linn. Sp. Pl.* 1372. *Jacq. Hort. Schönbr. v.* 2. *p.* 29. *t.* 184–185. *Flora Flumin. v.* 9. *t.* 117. *Willd. Sp. Pl. v.* 2. *p.* 289. *Hort. Kew. ed.* 2. *v.* 2. *p.* 336.

Calla Dracontium. *Mey. Esseq. p.* 197.

Calla pertusa. *Kunth, Syn. v.* 1. *p.* 129.

Dracontium, foliis pertusis, caule scandente. *Miller, Gard. Dict. v.* 1; *Ic. t.* 296.

Arum hederaceum, amplis foliis perforatis. *Plum. Amer. v.* 40. *t.* 56–57.

The genus *Monstera* was established by Adanson upon this plant, the *Dracontium pertusum* of Linnæus, and adopted by the distinguished writer on *Aroideæ*, Dr. Schott, whose generic character we have adopted, and who, in his 'Meletemata Botanica,' united with it the *Arum ligulatum*, Auct., and *Pothos cannæfolia*, Rudge. Afterwards, in his 'Synopsis Aroidearum,' he separated the two latter genera, and referred them to *Philodendron*. Pœppig and Endlicher, however, and Miquel and Gardner and Liebmann, have each given a new species to *Monstera:* how far all of them may correspond with Schott's views of the genus, I have no means of knowing. The plant is a native of tropical America and the West Indian Islands, and has been introduced into English gardens more than a century ago, namely, in 1752, by Mr. Philip Miller.

Descr. It is a scandent *plant*, several feet in length, running up the trunks of trees, and attaching itself to their bark by thick fleshy fibres. The main *stem* or trunk is one or two inches thick, but variable in size in different parts of the same stem, ringed, as it were, with the scars formed by fallen leaves, more or less branched; the *branches* are narrowed at the base, leafy. *Leaves* distichous, long-petioled, from a span to a foot long, oblique at the base, acuminulate at the apex, somewhat waved at the margin, dark-green, glossy, with stout costa, penni-veined, entire or in the disc and between the veins more or less perforated with large linear or oblong openings, one between each pair of veins, at various and very uncertain distances from the costa, lying parallel with the veins. *Petioles* grooved, with a membranous and sheathing margin, auricled above. *Bracteæ* elongated, boat-shaped, green, terminal from between the most superior pair of leaves: from this bract the *peduncle* emerges, thick, terete. *Spatha* cream-colour, deep cymbiform, ovate, acute: in the inside the surface appears as if impressed with the flowers of the spadix. *Peduncle* not much exserted beyond the bractea. *Spadix* included, much shorter than the spatha, cylindrical, thick, obtuse, clothed with white pistils for its whole length, which are closely compacted; those towards the base without stamens, the rest surrounded by seven *stamens*, which are close-pressed. *Filaments* broad, plane, tipped with two-celled *anthers*. *Ovary* turbinate, tapering upwards into a short *style*, two-celled, four-seeded. *Stigma* minute, four-lobed.

Fig. 1. Single stamen. 2. Pistil from the upper part of the spadix, surrounded by its stamens. 3. Vertical section of the pistil. 4. Transverse section:—*magnified*.

5087.

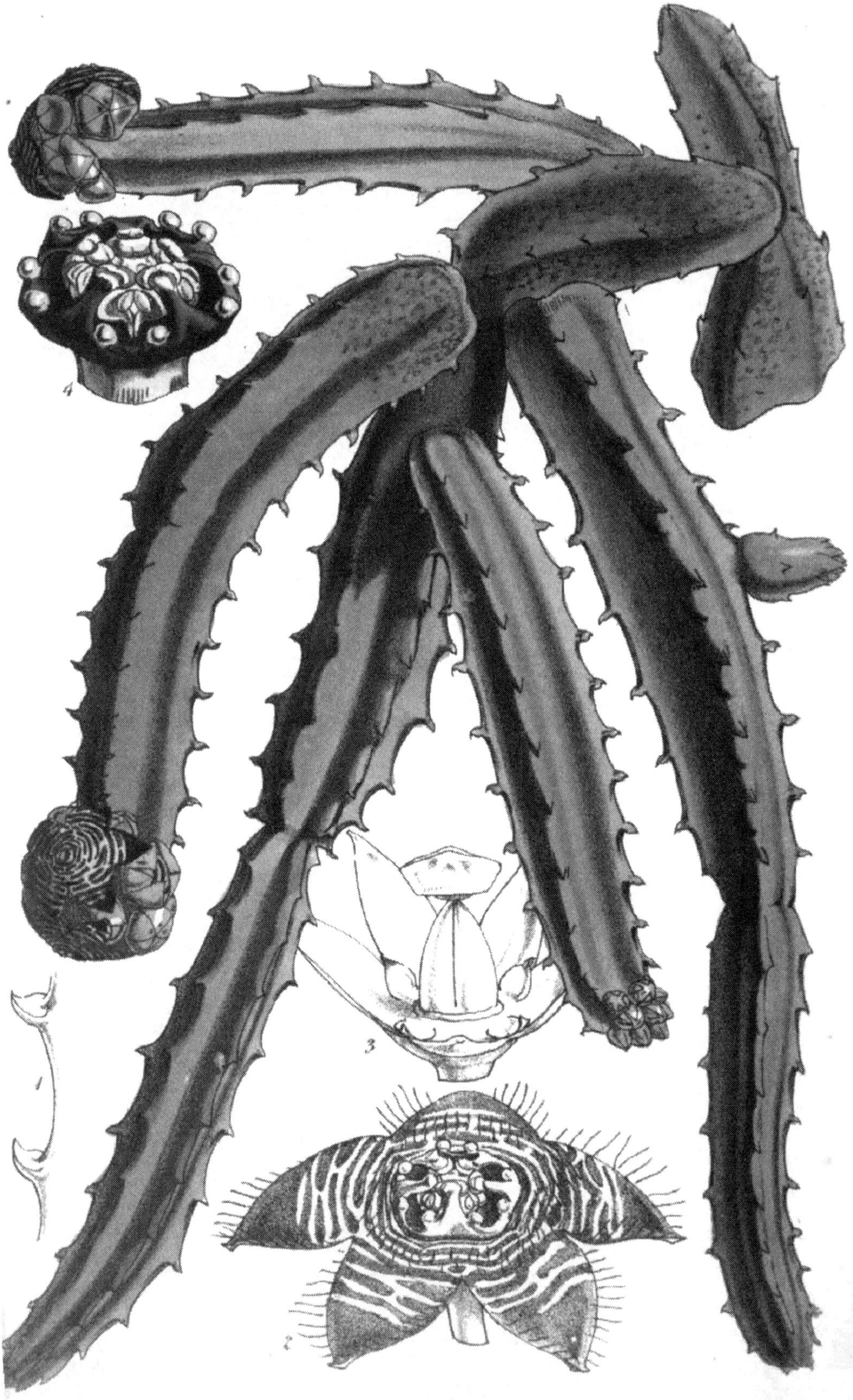

Tab. 5087.

APTERANTHES Gussoniana.

Gussoni's Apteranthes.

Nat. Ord. Asclepiadeæ.—Pentandria Digynia.

Gen. Char. Calyx quinquepartitus. *Corolla* rotata, quinquefida; *laciniis* late ovatis, apice pilosis. *Gynostegium* faucem subæquans. *Corona* staminea simplex, quinqueloba; *lobis* subtriangularibus, obtusis, stigmate incumbentibus, carnosulis, basi et a latere globulis obtusis flavis stipatis. *Antheræ* apice simplices; *massæ pollinis* rotundatæ, margine hinc pellucidæ. *Stigma* muticum. *Folliculi* . . .—Herbæ Stapeliæ *habitu, in regione Mediterranea occidentali*, ramis *tetragonis dentatis*, floribus *umbellatis parvis rufo-fuscis transverse rugosis, ad faucem pilis raris inspersis inodoris. De Cand.*

Apteranthes *Gussoniana.*

Apteranthes Gussoniana. *Mikan, Act. Acad. Nat. Cur. v.* 17. *p.* 594. *t.* 41. "*Gussoni, Notiz.* 1832, *n.* 87, *cum ic.*" *De Cand. Prodr. v.* 8. *p.* 649. *Cosson et Dur. Fl. Alger. t.* 62. *f.* 1 (*sine descript.*).

Stapelia Gussoniana. *Jacq. in Bot. Reg. t.* 1731.

Stapelia Europæa. *Guss. Act. Soc. Borb. v.* 4. *p.* 81, *et Suppl. p.* 65. *Flor. Siculæ, v.* 1. *p.* 288.

Bircherosia Munbyana, "*Decaisne in litt.*" (*ad cl. Mnnby*), *Menby, Fl. d'Alger, p.* 25.

Formerly, Asclepiadeous plants, with the habit of the well-known genus *Stapelia*, were supposed to be peculiar to the deserts of southern Africa; but we have now, of this group, the genus *Caralluma*, of which two species are peculiar to the East Indies, one to Arabia; *Boucerosia*, whose nine species are found in the East Indies, Arabia, Senegambia; and *Apteranthes*, the plant now under consideration, the most interesting of all in a geographical point of view, inasmuch as it is the only representative of the group which extends to Europe. It was first, before 1832, detected by Professor Gussoni, on the Sicilian island of Lampedusa; has since been found about Oran, in Algeria, by an English botanist resident there, Mr. Munby; and more recently in saline places at Cape Gata, and at Almeria, in Spain, by Mr. Webb. A solitary species only is known of the genus, for "*Apteranthes Numidica*, Durieu, Explor. Alger. t. 62," of Pritzel's valuable 'Iconum Botanicarum Index locupletissimus,' should have been *Campanula Numidica*, which is the name written and the plant referred to on the plate quoted. Our greenhouse owes the possession of this rarity to Mr. Munby, I believe its discoverer in North Africa, unless the *Stapelia hirsuta* of Desfontaines, Fl. Atlantica, vol. i. p. 213;—surely it cannot be the South African *St. hirsuta*, Linn., although Desfontaines considered it as such. It flowers with us in September.

Descr. The entire aspect of the plant is that of a small-flowered *Stapelia;* the *stems* and more or less pendent *branches* are quite leafless, about as thick as one's finger, with from four to six angles, more or less deeply channelled between the angles, and these dentate, at intervals of nearly half an inch from each other, with short, sharp, triangular *teeth*, which are convex below, plane above. *Flowers* small, in *umbels* springing from the apex of a branch, or from a little below the apex, five to seven or eight in an umbel. *Pedicels* very short. *Calyx* quinquepartite; segments lanceolate, acute, spreading; within, at each sinus, are five small ovato-acute scales, only seen on removing the corolla. *Corolla* scarcely three-quarters of an inch broad, rotate, fleshy, pale-yellow, mottled and banded with dingy-purple, the five ovate segments soon recurved, villous at the faux and at the margins. *Gynostegium* sunk in the short tube of the corolla, five-lobed at the margin; the lobes dark-purple, triangular, its apex two-lobed, yellow: and there are two bright-yellow globose *glands* at the base. These lobes are close-pressed upon the stigma. *Anthers* simple at the apex. *Stigma* a depressed, obscurely five-angled, large, peltate disc.

Fig. 1. Teeth, from the angles of the stem. 2. Flower. 3. Portion of calyx and pistil. 4. Gynostegium:—*magnified*.

5088.

W. Fitch, del. et lith.

Vincent Brooks, Imp.

Tab. 5088.

LOBELIA trigonocaulis.

Triangular-stemmed Lobelia.

Nat. Ord. Lobeliaceæ.—Pentandria Monogynia.

Gen. Char. Calyx tubo obconico, turbinato v. hemisphærico, cum ovario connato; *limbo* supero, quinquefido. *Corolla* summo calycis tubo inserta, tubulosa, *tubo* hinc apice fisso; *limbi* quinquefidi uni-bilabiati *laciniis* tribus inferioribus pendulis, duabus superioribus pendulis v. cum inferioribus conniventibus. *Stamina* 3, cum corolla inserta; *filamenta* et *antheræ*, omnes v. saltim duæ inferiores barbatæ, in tubum connatæ. *Ovarium* inferum, vertice brevissime exsertum, bi-triloculare. *Ovula* in placentis carnosulis, dissepimento utrinque adnatis v. e loculorum angulo centrali porrectis, plurima, anatropa. *Stylus* inclusus; *stigma* demum exsertum, bilobum; *lobis* divaricatis, orbiculatis, subtus pilorum annulo cinctis. *Capsula* bi-trilocularis, ultra verticem exsertum, loculicido-bi-trivalvis, *Semina* plurima, minima, scrobiculata. *Embryo* in axi albuminis carnosi orthotropus; *cotyledonibus* brevissimis, obtusis; *radicula* umbilica proxima, centripeta. —Herbæ *perennes, v. rarius annuæ, in regionibus tropicis subtropicisque totius orbis observatæ, in America æquinoctiali imprimis copiosæ, in Europa media rarissimæ,* habitu *et* inflorescentia *admodum variæ. Endl.*

Lobelia *trigonocaulis;* glabra decumbens, caule ramoso trigono sulcato, foliis ovatis nunc subcordatis inæqualiter dentato-laciniatis subpinnatifidis in petiolum alatum æquilongum attenuatis supremis angustis, racemis terminalibus foliosis remotifloris, floribus declinatis, pedicellis filiformibus bracteatis, calycis laciniis linearibus ovario longioribus, capsulis maturis subglobosis ("semiovatis") nutantibus.

Lobelia trigonocaulis. *F. Mueller, Fragm. Phytogr. Austral. v.* 1. *p.* 19.

The genus *Lobelia*, though much diminished in number of species by the separation of new genera from it, is nevertheless still very numerous in individuals. Of these Australia has its fair proportion. The present is an addition to those already known, and seems peculiar to North-east Australia. Dr. F. Mueller gives Brisbane river as the locality, on the authority of Mr. Hill and himself. Messrs. Hugh Low and Son, of the Clapton Nursery, possess living plants reared from seeds sent by Mr. Hill from Mount Lindsay, Moreton Bay, and these (from which our figure is taken) show it to be a very ornamental plant, and one well calculated for "bedding out" in open borders, where blue flowers are such a desideratum. The brightness of the colour

December 1st, 1858.

is here much enhanced by the large white spot on the lower lip and the red tinge on the tube.

Descr. A rather small, decumbent, herbaceous, glabrous *plant*, with a perennial *root* (according to Dr. Mueller), and triangular and furrowed *stems* and *branches*. *Leaves* rather distant, an inch to an inch and a half long, ovate, deeply toothed and laciniated (sometimes almost cordate), tapering into a winged petiole about equal in length with the blade; upper ones gradually smaller and narrower, and almost entire. *Racemes* terminal, leafy; *pedicels* distant, erect, filiform, bearing one or two linear *bracts*. *Flower* declined, not inaptly resembling a Violet. *Calyx-segments* linear, as long as the broad ovate ovary. *Corolla* blue, variegated with white, and a red tinge upon the cleft tube above. *Capsule* semiglobose, drooping.

Fig. 1. Front view of a flower. 2. Side view of ditto:—*magnified*.

W. Fitch, delt et lith.

Vincent Brooks, Imp.

Tab. 5089.

FIELDIA australis.

Australian Fieldia.

Nat. Ord. Cyrtandraceæ.—Didynamia Angiospermia.

Gen. Char. Calyx 5-partitus, persistens, *lobis* lanceolato-linearibus, *bractea* spathacea ovata acuta bifida lateraliter stipatus. *Corolla* tubuloso-ventricosa; *limbo* quinquefido, æquali, subbilabiato. *Stamina* 4, fertilia, vix didynama, cum quinto sterili dimidio breviore. *Antheræ* globoso-didynamæ, biloculares, loculis parallelis. *Stigma* bilamellatum. *Bacca* spongiosa, subcarnosa, ovata, 1-locularis, loculis parallelis. *Placentæ* duæ, carnosæ, in laminas recurvas lateraliter productæ. *Semina* plurima, parva, nidulantia, ovato-oblonga, aptera.—Suffrutex *radicans, pseudo-parasiticus, ramosus,* ramulis *ferrugineo-velutinis.* Folia *opposita, valde cujusque jugi inæqualia, remota, breviter petiolata, basi cuneata, superne cuneato-serrata.* Pedicelli *axillares, uniflori.* Flores *nutantes, ex albo subvirescentes. De Cand.*

Fieldia *australis.*

Fieldia australis. *All. Cunn. in Field's Mem. of N. S. Wales, p.* 364 (*with a figure*). *Hook. Exot. Flora, p.* 232. *t.* 232. *De Cand. Prod. v.* 9. *p.* 286.

Basyleophyta Frederici-Augusti. *F. Muell.* 1*st Rep. on the Bot. of Victoria, p.* 16.

This little-known and singular plant is a native of the Blue Mountains of New South Wales, where it was first detected by Mr. Caley, in 1804, and afterwards by Mr. Allan Cunningham, who dedicated it to his excellent friend the late Barron Field, Esq., Judge of the Supreme Court of New South Wales. It was to the same gentleman that Gaudichaud afterwards, namely in 1826, dedicated another plant, one of the *Orchideæ.** Our plant has also been gathered at Gipps's Land by Dr. F. Mueller, at Shoal Haven, New South Wales, by Mr. Backhouse, and at Fives' Island, by Mr. Bynoe. We were so fortunate, in 1857, as to receive living plants from Mr. Moore of the Sydney Botanical Garden, which flowered copiously in the greenhouse in September, 1858. Its habit is peculiar for a Cyrtandraceous plant, and it has perhaps as strong a claim to rank with the

* *Vandalissochiloides,* Lindl.

Bignoniaceæ as with the *Crytandraceæ*, in which latter the species are usually herbaceous.

Descr. This has a straggling, woody *stem* and *branches*, somewhat climbing, and rooting on the rough bark or among moss, villous with short fulvous hairs, or more or less downy. *Leaves* opposite, remote, unequal in size, a small one frequently being opposed to the larger one, ovate or ovato-lanceolate, downy, acuminate, shortly petiolate, coarsely serrated, entire at the base, paler and more villous beneath. *Veins* pinnated, rather obscure. *Peduncles* axillary, solitary, nearly an inch long, bearing a solitary pendulous flower; the apex, beneath the calyx, swollen, and having a spathæform *bract* on one side, deeply cut into two equal lanceolate segments. *Calyx* deeply cut into five linear-lanceolate, erect, downy *segments*. *Corolla* an inch and a half or nearly two inches long, tubuloso-cylindrical, downy, pale yellowish-green, the limb short, equal, cut into five, rounded, spreading *segments*. *Stamens* four, arising from the very base of the tube. *Filaments* as long as the tube of the corolla. *Anthers* subglobose. There is a fifth small *abortive stamen*. *Ovary* ovate, arising from a glandular *annulus*, two-celled, many-seeded. *Style* as long as the corolla. *Stigma* small, unequally two-cleft.

Fig. 1. Corolla laid open, showing the stamens. 2. Stamen. 3. Pistil. 4. Transverse section of ovary:—*magnified*.

5090.
3
2.
1
Vincent Brooks Imp.

Tab. 5090.

BILLBERGIA Liboniana.

Libon's Billbergia.

Nat. Ord. Bromeliaceæ.—Hexandria Monogynia.

Gen. Char. (*Vide supra*, Tab. 4756.)

Billbergia *Liboniana;* surculosa, foliis radicalibus ligulatis acutis mucronatis margine serrulatis supra læte viridibus subtus obscure albido-furfuraceis, scapo erecto bracteato, bracteis subulatis appressis, spica laxa 6–10-floro, floribus erectis, sepalis erectis rubris, petalis calyce duplo longioribus erectis lineari-oblongis intense purpureo-cæruleis basi albidis intus laminis duabus elongatis apice dentatis instructis et ad basin squamis duabus obovatis longe fimbriatis.

Billbergia Liboniana. *De Jonghe, Journ. d'Hort. Prat. Mars*, 1851, *cum icone. Lem. Jard. Fleur. v.* 3. *p.* 197. *Planch. Flore des Serres, v.* 10. *p.* 195, *cum ic.*

Received at Kew from the Belgian gardens, where it is stated to have been introduced from the vicinity of Rio de Janeiro, by "le voyageur naturaliste Libon," after whom it has received its specific name. It is a plant of some beauty, and is another plant added to those *Bromeliaceæ* which are highly deserving of cultivation in our hothouses. Where the collection of these (in amount of species, we mean) is considerable, some or other is in flower at all seasons of the year, and not a few in the depth of winter. The drawing was taken from a plant in Kew Gardens, which flowered in August, 1858.

Descr. The species is small in stature, compared to many of the *Bromeliaceæ*, scarcely more than a foot in height, independent of the scape. The plant is sarmentose, and these runners, by which the species is easily increased, are nearly half an inch thick, terete, scaly with small, rigid, broad, subulate, spinescent, abortive leaves. From these runners tufts of foliage arise, with no visible stem: the lowest ones are squamiform, like those of the runners; the inner become gradually larger, a foot long, ligulate, the sides convolute, mucronately acuminate at the apex, the margin spinescently serrated, the upper or inner side of the leaf is dark-green, the outer paler from a whitish furfuraceous substance with which it is more or less invested. *Scape* arising from the centre of the foliage, and scarcely exceeding it in length, erect or nearly so, rather slender, bracteated with long, subulate, erect, rigid bracts, becoming shorter in the inflorescence. *Spike* lax, of from five to twelve erecto-patent flowers. *Sepals* oblong, erect, appressed, imbricate, acute, red, with a paler streak. *Petals* twice as long as the calyx, white below, the rest deep purple-blue, linear-oblong, obtuse, erect, straight, the sides convolute, with two linear laminæ within, almost as long as the petals, toothed at the apex; and two small scales at the base, long-fringed. *Filaments* inserted just above the laminæ, two on each petal. *Ovary* terete, inferior. *Style* shorter than the petals. *Stigma* three-lobed.

Fig. 1. Flower. 2. Petal, with two stamens, laminæ, and scales. 3. Pistil:—*magnified.*

INDEX,

In which the Latin Names of the Plants contained in the Fourteenth Volume of the THIRD SERIES (or Eighty-fourth Volume of the Work) are alphabetically arranged.

INDEX,

In which the English Names of the Plants contained in the Fourteenth Volume of the THIRD SERIES (or Eighty-fourth Volume of the Work) are alphabetically arranged.

CPSIA information can be obtained
at www.ICGtesting.com
Printed in the USA
BVHW050205120621
609157BV00006B/222